TOWARD A DEEPER MEDITATION

TOWARD A DEEPER MEDITATION

Rejuvenating the Body
Illuminating the Mind
Experiencing the Spirit

By

Edgar Cayce and

John Van Auken

ARE
PRESS

ASSOCIATION FOR
RESEARCH AND
ENLIGHTENMENT

A.R.E. Press • Virginia Beach • Virginia

A.R.E. Press
215 67th Street
Virginia Beach, VA 23451–2061

Library of Congress Cataloging–in–Publication Data
Cayce, Edgar, 1877–1945.
Toward a deeper meditation : rejuvenating the body, illuminating
the mind, experiencing the spirit / by Edgar Cayce and John Van
Auken.–[Rev. & updated ed.].
    p.   cm.
ISBN 13: 978–0–87604–527–5 (trade pbk.)
1. Spiritual life. 2. Cayce, Edgar, 1877–1945. 3. Association for Research
and Enlightenment. I. Van Auken, John II. Van Auken, John. Spiritual
breakthrough. III. Title.
BP605.A77C39 2007
204—dc22

2007003845

Cover design by Richard Boyle

Contents

Foreword

*M*y coauthor, Edgar Cayce, passed away some years ago, but his enlightened contribution toward a greater understanding of meditation, both in concept and technique, continues strong today. He may be better known for his insights into holistic medicine and is credited by the *Journal of the American Medical Association* as the "father of the holistic movement" in America. He is also known for his call for more study into the purpose and process of dreaming, the need for a greater understanding of ancient civilizations, and improved harmony with the ecosystem we live in. But without a doubt, one of his most significant contributions came with his insistence that all people could enjoy improved personal spirituality and mental enlightenment by adding meditation to their daily lives.

I have worked with his meditation insights and instructions for nearly forty years and have taught and written about them for thirty years.

Edgar Cayce said: "There are *definite* conditions that arise from within the inner person when an individual enters into true or deep meditation. A physical condition happens, a physical activity takes place! Acting through what? Through that humanity has chosen to call the imaginative or the impulsive, and the sources of impulse are aroused by the shutting out of thought pertaining to activities of the carnal forces of a person. Changes naturally take place when there is the arousing of that stimuli *within* the individual that has within it the seat of the soul's dwelling, within the individual body of the person, and then this partakes of the individuality [the soul] rather than the personality." (281–13)

All of my coauthor's insights were dictated to his stenographer while he was in a deep, meditative state of consciousness. She filed them using a numbering system. Each discourse was given a number, usually associated with the person or group requesting the information, followed by a dash number that indicated how many discourses they had received. For example, the comment quoted above was given to a group seeking to improve their spiritual healing abilities. This group was given the number 281, and the discourse above was their thirteenth, thus the filing number 281–13.*

His stenographer was often surprised that Cayce's mind could dictate his comments and at the same time correct her shorthand spelling or clarify some detail for her! It was as if his mind were aware of what she was taking down in shorthand and of her thoughts about the content.

Cayce himself is a wonderful example of how profoundly meditation can help us and those we share our lives with.

In this latest book, Edgar Cayce and I present both the spirit and the mechanism for effective and relevant meditation in daily life. We cover classical and modern concepts and techniques, the fundamentals and advanced nuances, and provide perspectives and tips on both the method and the experience.

John Van Auken, Director
Association for Research and Enlightenment, Inc.

---

*Since the language of the Cayce discourses is somewhat similar to the language of the King James Bible, I have slightly paraphrased some of the quotes for clarity.

Section One

FUNDAMENTAL CONCEPTS

Sanctuary

*O*ne of the most pleasant activities of personal spirituality is sitting quietly in the sanctuary of one's temple while aware of the life force flowing through you. Nothing compares to it. As Edgar Cayce noted during one of his deep attunements to the mind of the Maker, "If you will but open your tabernacle of consciousness to allow the holy to come in and sup with you, all the beauties of peace and harmony are yours—for they are the birthright of each soul." (Reading 987-4; as you may know, for privacy the reading numbers replace people's names.)

On a recent night, I awoke about two in the morning, feeling surprisingly refreshed from only four hours' sleep. I went to my meditation spot and began to meditate in the dark. The meditation easily moved from normal, self-conscious aloneness into a sense of the presence of the infinite consciousness, and then into a oneness with all life. I was surprised, because my daily life had been unusually rocky lately, with much turmoil and tension. But in the wee hours of this night, all was quiet and the world outside of me was still.

I began the meditation by surrounding my body, mind, and soul with an imaginary shield that blocked out external influences. On this particular night, it wasn't difficult. The neighborhood and house were quiet. My personal, outer mind seemed unusually quiet too.

To help shield me, I used a variation of one of Edgar Cayce's prayers of protection. Something like this: "Now as I approach the throne of power, might, grace, and mercy, I wrap about myself the protection found in a love for God–consciousness, in the thought of Christ Consciousness." Then I strived to *see* and *feel* this happening. After only a few repetitions of prayer, my shield was up. I felt surrounded by my love for God and the Infinite's consciousness of me. I was now in my "bubble," secure from *external* distractions.

Since I was using Edgar Cayce's method for making passage through dimensions of consciousness (more on this method later), the next step was to intentionally remove the "earthly portion and personality" from my body, suspending it outside of me. This is how we protect ourselves from *internal* distractions. It also makes for a purer meditation, because the earthly self has little to no influence over the experience. Removing the earthly portions of oneself and the personality is done using the *imagination* and the *will*. I simply imagine my personal, earthly self and all its concerns sitting outside of my body, quietly. And I use my will to prevent it from regaining control during the meditation. As with so many meditation techniques, this one takes repetition before one feels results. Once the earthly portion and personality are removed, suspended in front of me, I am left with a strange but pleasant sensation of emptiness and lightness within my body.

When I first began using this technique, I used to be surprised that there was anything left of me once the earthly portion and personality were removed! But, as Cayce so often taught, the real you and me is a quiet giant of a companion to the personal, outer self—in the same manner and proportion as the whole of an iceberg is to its exposed tip. What you and I see and know of ourselves is a very tiny portion of the whole self. Our soul–self lies behind the surface of consciousness and behind the external senses. Fortunately, our little outer-self can be suspended for a time, and our deeper soul–self can awaken and rise to consciousness and predominance.

At 2 a.m. it is much easier to remove the earthly portion and personality, because they really don't want to be up! I had an easy time on this night. Cayce taught that it was an excellent time to meditate, explaining (his parenthetical comment): "The body–mind (if it has slept) is in that vibration where it is between the physical, the mental, and spiritual activities. If it is kept awake, it isn't a good time to meditate, but sleep, and then arise, and *purposefully*, use this time when the triune self is balanced." (1861-19; also see 3051-7)

Now, with my earthly portion and personality suspended in front of me, my body felt open, empty, and quiet.

The next step in the method is to "subjugate control to my subconscious and soul," as Cayce directed both himself and those seeking to duplicate his journey. Now this takes a lot of imagination and some understanding of how we are arranged. The personality and earthly portion are in charge of our central nervous system, the five senses, and the conscious mind. But since we are meditating, the central nervous system, five senses, and conscious mind are almost completely shut down. We are not moving, not attempting to perceive with any of our senses, and are still and quiet, as far as outer life is concerned. And yet the body remains alive—breathing, circulating blood, adjusting hormonal messages, and so on. And a degree of consciousness is still present. The life force is now controlled more by the deeper autonomic nervous system than the central, which Cayce often referred to as the "sympathetics." And the consciousness we now feel is the fringe of the vast subconscious mind, a portion of which is our dreaming mind.

Cayce explained that the subconscious mind is the *bridge* from the physical outer world to the metaphysical inner worlds and our spirit. Therefore, this important stage in the meditation is where we yield control to our subconscious and that part of our self that is our soul. Again, in the early years of this practice, one has to use the imagination in order to perceive the soul-self. But as one grows in the practice, the soul-self becomes a familiar aspect of one's whole being—a portion of what Cayce called the "entity."

As I did this on that night, I felt myself slip deeper and deeper into stillness. At first, my breathing was deep and rhythmical. As the quietness settled in and the stillness became profound, my breathing became shallow. I was hardly breathing at all.

The next step in this Cayce method is to give your subconscious mind a suggestion that will lead you into the Spirit and the infinite, universal consciousness. If not done at this time, the meditation will drift into a watery wandering from which we will eventually awaken,

feeling drowsy and dull. I've experienced this many times. It is an indication that one did not achieve the level of meditation that Cayce encouraged. But if we give our subconscious a direct suggestion, it will
lead to an inspiring and energizing meditation from which we will
awaken feeling a personal connection with the Life Force. The little "I
am" makes contact with the great "I AM." This contact makes the whole
of our being feel good and happy—at least until earth life drains the
power of the experience from us and we need to seek the connection all
over again.

To guide my subconscious into the realms of the superconscious and
on into the infinite, universal consciousness, I use variations of this
suggestion: "Arise my soul and enter into the infinite, universal mind
and spirit." As I repeat this suggestion, I strive to *feel* and imagine it
happening. I imagine myself rising and expanding from out of my little
point of consciousness into the infinite, universal mind and spirit, into
what Cayce often called God–consciousness. I repeat the process over
and over until I fully feel myself levitated and expanded into the vast,
infinite presence of the creative forces and consciousness of the universe. On this night, the presence of God–consciousness was particularly strong and clear. Mildly exhilarating vibrations enlivened my body
and mind during the time of at–onement with the Infinite. I felt peace
and contentment and that all things flow toward goodness, ultimately—
despite my outer life's challenges at this time.

It's important to realize that I am not out of my body, as you might
think. In fact, Cayce specifically taught practitioners not to go out of
their bodies during this practice. Rather, he wanted us to go through
"dimensions of consciousness" in our minds. Therefore, when I am in
at–onement with the Infinite, it feels like a gigantic V of energy and
contact, with the bottom of the V being where my body is, and the top
of the V being where my consciousness is—in the endless vastness of
infinite, universal consciousness. Abiding in God's consciousness is, as
Jesus described it, like "supping" with our Father and Mother after a
long absence. It's gentle. It's loving. It's nourishing. Sometimes there is
real information conveyed. But most of the time, it is simply a gentle
togetherness, with the information and guidance coming later, as a natural outcome of spending time together. I've found that deep, quiet medi-

tations often end quietly with no great information or instruction. But later, usually through my dreams but occasionally through intuitive knowing, guidance and information come. Sometimes, however, the "supping" will produce immediate knowing and a subtle sense of direction.

On this night, I quietly enjoyed the company of my Maker and His/Her love for me and my family, friends, and coworkers.

The body is wonderfully arranged for both physical activity *and* metaphysical activity—yet few people ever experience it. The body is, as so many teachers have claimed throughout the ages, a temple of the living God. And, as with all temples (Hindu, Buddhist, Egyptian, Mayan, Hebrew, etc.), the body–mind temple is a sanctuary. This is where the real *communion* takes place. And the mind, the deeper mind, is the crucial link: "Your body is the temple of the living God, your mind the connecting and communicating link with the Divine, through which you may ever receive the answer, if you will but harken." (2174-2) Let's take a moment to understand Cayce's perspective on the mind's role in communing with God. All of the following insights come from his discourses in reading 281-13, but I've edited it for clarity and focus to our point at hand:

"There are definite conditions that arise within the inner person when an individual enters into true or deep meditation. The sources of impulse and imagination are aroused by the shutting out of thought pertaining to the carnal forces of the person. Then, [the person] partakes of the individuality [the soul] rather than the personality [the outer self]. If the image that is raised by the individual in its imaginative and impulse force [motivation] takes the form of the ideal held to be raised to, then the individual bears the mark of the Lamb, or the Christ, of the Holy One, or the Son, or *any* of the names we may have given to that which enables the individual to enter *through* it into the very presence of the Creative Forces. The soul is within its temple, within the body of the individual, see? With the arousing then of this image, it rises along that which is known as . . . the pineal center, to the base of the brain, then to the hidden eye in the center of the brain system." (Much more on this in later chapters.)

Clearly, imagination, imagery, and motivation are important ingredients in Cayce's method. I have found that my imagery has changed over the many years I've been practicing this specific meditative method. Think of these images as furnishings for your sanctuary. These will be unique to each soul's experiences, beliefs, and ideals. What is *God* and *heavenly* is going to differ according to the mind that is seeking. At least, in the *beginning* this is correct. In the beginning, imagery may provide you with initial furnishings that reflect your personal perspective on spirituality and God–consciousness, and they will provide you with just the surroundings you need for your communion with God.

In my case, the first imagery was of a long, vertical shaft, reaching from the top of my head into the many dimensions of heavenly realms. At the top of the shaft, the opening to the heavens, the "water of life" was flowing down into that shaft. When I would finally arrive at this place, I would lie in a flowing pool of this heavenly water on a plateau surrounding the opening. The water rejuvenated me. I enjoyed lying in it and feeling its revivifying energy. Much of my meditation time was spent lying in this flowing water. Occasionally, off in the distance, I could see a sun that seemed very far away, and there was a chasm between my plateau and another plateau nearer to that sun. But I was content to be where I was. Somehow I knew that I needed more time in these waters before attempting to travel toward that sun. But these initial images and concepts were special to me, to my soul. While giving one of his famous readings, the individual mind of the *man* Edgar Cayce experienced images of himself traveling in a bubble through deep, vast water to reach the higher realms. Cayce gave one of his famous readings on this imagery (254–68), and though the answer was complex, covering over four pages, it was profound. Let me try to summarize and paraphrase it for our purposes here:

"In order to bring some understanding of what a soul may pass through when traveling from one realm to another, it becomes necessary to convey the experiences in images and concepts that are comprehensible to those souls in the lower realm—in this case, in the earth realm. Since Cayce must travel through many realms of thought, symbolized by the water, and return with names, dates, and ages intact, what better way to convey this than traveling in a bubble through massive amounts of water. The body acts as the bubble for the soul while incarnate in the earth dimensions. When traveling beyond the earth, the bubble symbolizes a vessel that protects the soul on its journey to and from the place where the records are kept. Cayce sees here the Book of Life for each soul as well as the keeper of the records—but these are also symbols. A mind that thinks books, needs books! One that thinks of heaven as 'Elysian Fields' needs birds and flowers. One must find the *materialized form* of that portion of the Maker that that entity, that soul, can enjoy and comprehend. Houses built in the woods would appeal to some. Woods, in its essence, are what? Books, in their essence, are what? What is the more real, the book with its printed pages, its gilt edges, or the *essence* of that told in the book? Which is the more real, the love manifested in the Savior for His brethren, or the essence of love that may be seen even in the vilest of passion? They are one. But they bring this into being in a *materialized form* by the combining of elements of the one source to produce a materialization. Beautiful, isn't it? Only those who become conscious of the *essence* and have attuned themselves to that which is in accord with His will may know. For each soul, every soul, should seek to attune its mind, its soul to the Mother–Father God in Jesus the Christ. Tune into that light, and it becomes *beautiful* in that you think, that you are, that you live!"

Cayce is acknowledging that the imagery of souls varies greatly. Whatever *you* experience as "furnishings" for your sanctuary is *right for you*.

As the years passed, my imagery changed dramatically, from visual scenes to simply *feelings*. I had sensations of rising and expanding, and a deep sense of at-onement with the Universal Consciousness, with God's presence and mind. Gradually, visual images faded to pure feelings, or the essences, of everything. At first, I became concerned about this. But then I came across Cayce readings that acknowledge the value of subtle feelings or knowing something without dramatic images or phenomena, as from out of nowhere.

On this particular night, my imagery was minimal. I mostly felt the upward and expanding movement from finite self into infinite God-consciousness. I did have a *sensation* of my heavenly "Parents" embracing me and holding me for the duration of the communion. And while in this sacred space, I felt renewed, my faith strengthened, my trust in ultimate good renewed, my sense of well-founded trust in the unseen forces of life restored. Having lived a lot of life, I knew that physical life would consume these wonderful energies eventually and that I would have to come back here again and again in order to maintain these feelings while living an incarnate life. It's just the nature of the earth realm and personal consciousness.

As I said, my outer, earthly life was particularly challenging during the time leading up to this evening's meditation. Was the good meditation a salve for my weariness and wounds? Was it a gift from a merciful Creator? Or was my outer self so fatigued that it surrendered more completely to my inner self, allowing the better attunement to the infinite, universal consciousness? It reminded me of the reading saying that even in hard times God will come: "There may be raised within self that consciousness of the at-onement with the spiritual forces that may revivify, regenerate, arouse that of health and happiness *even under adverse conditions in materiality."* (618-3, my italics)

If it were not for these moments with the Life Force and Universal Consciousness, I would not have endured many of the lessons that my particular personality needed to learn or face the tests of this incarnation. I wouldn't have had the staying power or the depth of trust in God, and certainly not the patience to keep on keeping on in hard times. As Cayce once noted: "Know that your body-mind is indeed the temple of the living God. Thus may you find often that upon the horns of the altar *within you* many of the burdens may be laid aside, and that the sweet incense of faith and hope and prudence and patience will arise to bring the consciousness and the awakening of the glories that may be yours." (1472-1)

I have practiced this technique many times, but this night the sanctuary felt like a spatial orb of protection and privacy, a sacred bubble within which my soul and its Maker communed silently. When we have budgeted the time allotted to us to include some personal, spiritual communing with the Life Force and the Universal Consciousness, then our temple is a warm, ever-ready sanctuary waiting to be enjoyed—doors open, lights on, and our heavenly Mother and Father waiting. As the Spirit of God promised in the book of the Revelation, 3:20: "Behold, I stand at the door and knock; if anyone hears my voice and opens the door, I will come in to him, and will sup with him, and he with me."

2

Sabbath: The Intermission

As scientists look out into our universe, they see signs that cosmic life exploded out of a central, silent point in space. It is spreading out infinitely, in all manner of excitement and expression. According to ancient religions and myths, this expanding life explosion will, at some magic moment, turn back into itself. And stillness will reign again. Only for a time, because it will repeat the cycle, like the exhaling and inhaling of the Great Spirit of the Cosmos.

This is seen as the rhythm of life, and it is reflected in our little lives: we wake from the slumber of night, are active in the light of the day, then return to sleep—only to awake and do it all over again! It is the way and rhythm of life.

The contact point throughout all of this living and dying, waking and sleeping, is the silent, infinite womb from which Life always springs forth and to which it returns again and again. It is the place of original silence and stillness—the womb of God.

The *essence* of the commandment to keep holy the Sabbath is not simply about a day of the week but the intermission from life, from activity and self-consciousness. Sabbath literally means "intermission." The archangel Michael's secret name is Sabbathiel, meaning "Lord of the Intermission." Cayce's readings call Michael the "Lord of the Way." The intermission—the place and moment of stillness from which all life springs forth and to which it returns—is "the Way." And it is always there for us to touch, to experience.

The Taoist teacher Lü–tsu taught that the true way is action that leads to non–action. He said moments in non–action are rejuvenating moments in the "Elixir of Life," the essence and source of all life, and therefore "the true energy of the transcendent great One." He taught that lifetimes of karma are dissolved in just a few moments in this silent stillness.

Keeping holy the Sabbath is budgeting time for an intentional intermission from life, self–seeking, and self–consciousness. Meditation is a way to reconnect with and abide in this mystical place of the origin and destiny of all life.

As Cayce instructed in one of his psychic readings: "This is not for Sunday or for the Sabbath or for the new moon, or for some periods when there may be the turning away for the moment; for it is TODAY— 'if ye will hear my voice'—always, ever!" (615-1)

Each cycle of day and night is a reflection of the whole life cycle, in the great macrocosm and in the little microcosm of one's own life. Each day, a bit of time should be set aside for time in the silence, because in that silence is spiritual nourishment, mental enlightenment, and physical rejuvenation. The body and mind need nourishment and exercise each day, as does the soul and the spirit, though few ever think of these needs. Few activities bring more contentment than time set aside for the nourishment that comes from sitting or lying in the silence.

Now many would say that this type of nourishment can come from reading, reflecting, praying, or walking in a pleasant environment, but none of these compares to time spent in deep attunement to the source of one's life, the place from which all life sprang forth and to which all life will ultimately return.

The Trinity concept gives us an insight into the aspects of God and the phases of our relation to Him/Her. First, there is the parent, Mother–Father God; then there is the birth of the child, Son–Daughter of God; then there is the overarching Holy Spirit that brings all into oneness. Ultimately, there is only oneness, and we are, at our highest level of life, a part of that One.

Jesus shared with the woman at the well that the time for worshipping at her well or at his temple in Jerusalem was over. The time had come when the true worshippers of God would worship in spirit, for God is a Spirit and seeks our spirit in communion during the intermission from self-driven activity. Moments, however brief, in the stillness beyond activity, beyond self, bring us a peace and contentment that cannot be experienced any other way.

We need to budget time for an intermission of silent, centered, stillness with the source and destiny of life.

3

Paradise and Heaven

*I*n our many cultures and religions, from the East to the West, we humans have always told tales of a special place called Paradise. The word *pairidaeza* has its origins in the Avestan language of Zoroastrian teachings, in which it means a special "enclosure." In Greek, *paradeisos* means a unique "park." We associate this term with the original "park," the Garden of Eden, that special place where God walked and talked with us. On the cross, in his final moments, Jesus referred to this place when he told the thief who was dying next to him, "This day you will be with me in Paradise."

Paradise. The word means so much to us. It is a place of supreme happiness, exquisite beauty, perfect peace, and safety. It is where the righteous live after physical death.

In strict Christian teachings, however, paradise is not the ultimate resting stop for the deceased but an *intermediate* place for the departed souls of the righteous awaiting the final resurrection of the dead to eternal life with God and Christ. Cayce's readings support this *interim* view of Paradise. When he was asked what Jesus meant by his statement to the thief on the cross, Cayce answered: "The inter-between; the awareness of being in that state of transition between the material and the spiritual phases of consciousness of the Soul." (262-92)

Near death experiences (NDEs) have added to our understanding of

Paradise as an inter–between realm that can be known while still incarnate. Most who have had a NDE return to this world profoundly changed by the time in the inter–between, mostly in their outlook and attitude toward physical life and death.

Buddhists have a concept that also seems to separate the ultimate heavenly reality from an interim paradise. According to some of their key teachings, *nirvana*, which means ultimate bliss, is of such a nature as to render one who experiences nirvana useless in this world. It is a heavenly state so far from earthly reality that there is no connection between the two. However, *bodhisattva* consciousness, literally meaning "enlightened existence," is an interim state of consciousness of an advanced spiritual being who has chosen not to pass into full nirvana, choosing instead to continue in the round of rebirths in order to help others still in the body or even in the realms of life beyond bodily existence. Cayce appears to support this view of Paradise consciousness. During reading 5036–1 he answered a request to suggest a doctor who could carry out the recommended treatments, by saying, "There are those in Paradise who may work with these suggestions." It's good to know that there are healers in Paradise who can help others.

The Kingdom of Heaven

The Kingdom of Heaven is within us, Jesus taught, and he likened it to many things: to seed that a man sowed in his field, to leaven a woman hid in three measures of meal, to a treasure hidden in a field, to a pearl of great price, and to a net cast into the sea (see Matthew 13). Jesus said that one who has been made a disciple of the Kingdom of Heaven is like "a householder who brings forth out of his treasure things new and old." Cayce's readings say that the Kingdom of Heaven is attained through "the consciousness, the awareness of the activity of the spirit of truth in and through us, as individuals," and explain further that "the individual does not *go* to heaven, or paradise, or the universal consciousness, but it *grows* to same; through the use of self in those things that are virtues." (2505–1) Living in virtue and giving aid to others brings that happiness that is associated with the Kingdom of Heaven. It is a *growing* thing, like an unseen seed planted in good soil or unseen leaven kneaded into bread dough.

There is an implication in the Cayce work that as long as we are incarnate—in the body—we cannot *fully* realize or maintain a completely conscious connection with the Kingdom of Heaven. It's somewhat akin to the Buddhist idea of nirvana being so alien to this world as to be impossible to sustain while actively functioning here. In one of his readings, Cayce said that the spiritual entity and superconscious mind are a "thing apart from anything earthly" and can only be experienced by lifting oneself up into the spirit and higher levels of consciousness. He explained that "the earthly or material consciousness is ever tempered with material conditions; the superconsciousness with the consciousness between soul and spirit, partakes of the spiritual forces principally." He said that "we find only *projections* of subconscious and superconscious . . . in dreams and visions," unless we lift ourselves "into the superconscious forces," which are the higher spiritual forces and dimensions of our mind. Nevertheless, there is a connection between our earthly selves and our godly selves because the superconscious is affected by and helps affect our spiritual discernment and development, which occurs while we are in the earth realms and physical life. (900–16)

Heaven on Earth?

During one of his most inspired readings, Cayce said that we could know "heaven on earth or in the earth, or in flesh." It is the "destiny of those that are willing, who have had their minds, their bodies, their souls cleansed in the blood of the Lamb. How? By being as He, a living example of that He, the Christ, professed to be." (262–77) "Flesh and blood has not revealed this to you, but my Father which is in heaven. Heaven? Where? Within the hearts, the minds; the place where Truth is made manifest!" (262–87)

In the Revelation, a new heaven and a new earth are spoken of. Cayce stated that "as the desires, the purposes, the aims are to bring about the whole change physically, so does it create in the experience of each soul a new vision, a new comprehension. Is this not a new heaven, a new earth?" (281–37)

Heaven: A State of Mind or Place?

Some wonder if heaven is just a state of consciousness or an actual place. Some point to Jesus' comments to Mary in the garden after His resurrection, "Touch me not, for I have not ascended to my Father." Cayce addressed this: "Some would say this indicates that the heaven and the Father are somewhere else—a place of abode, the center about which all universal forces, all energies must turn. Heaven is that place, that awareness where the Soul—with all its attributes, its mind, and its body—becomes *aware* of being in the *presence* of the Creative Forces, one with same. That is heaven." (262-88)

4

The Trinity and Oneness

"*T*hey are one; as the Father, the Son and the Holy Spirit are one." Having stated this important principle, Cayce, from his deep trance state, then separates the Trinity into three distinct parts (2420–1):
1. God as the Father, Creator, Maker
2. The Son as the Way, the Mind, the Activity, the Preserver
3. The Holy Spirit as the motivative force—or as the destroyer or the maker alive

The first thing that strikes me after reading this is how perfectly it fits with ancient Hinduism, especially as Cayce identifies the Son with "the Preserver," and the Holy Spirit with "the destroyer." In classical Hinduism, God's three parts are:
1. Brahma, the Creator
2. Vishnu, the Preserver
3. Shiva, the Destroyer (of illusion and ignorance)

Shiva is often depicted sitting in meditation, with the water of life flowing from high on the mountaintop to a crescent moon on the crown of his head, a serpent is coiled around his neck (kundalini), a trident in one hand (power over negative forces), and his body is covered in ashes (indicating the need to die to physical gratifications in order to awaken to spiritual resources).

In another reading, Cayce differentiates the Trinity, using the microcosm of our composition: body, mind, and soul (1747–5):

1. Father–God is as the body, or the whole
2. Mind is as the Christ, which is the way
3. The Holy Spirit is as the soul, or—in material interpretation—purposes, hopes, desires

In the *macrocosm*, these would likely be *Father* as the Cosmos, *Son* as the Universal Consciousness, and *Holy Spirit* as the motivative force driving the Universe.

Returning to the *microcosm*, Cayce tries to help us grasp the difficult concept that physical life is a shadow of spiritual life. In this next reading, he develops this idea using Genesis (note: "these" refers to the parts of the Trinity):

> These, then, in self are a shadow of the spirit of the Creative Force. Thus the Father is as the body, the mind is as the Son, and the Soul is as the Holy Spirit. For it is eternal. It has ever been and ever will be, and it is the soul made in the image of the Creator, not merely the physical or mental being but with the attributes [of the Creator]. For, as is given in the beginning: God moved and said, "Let there be light," and there was light, not the light of the sun, but rather that of which, through which, in which every soul had, has, and ever has its being. For in truth you live and love and have your being in Him. "These considerations, then, each in analyzing of self, each has its part in your own physical consciousness, yes."   5246-1

In another reading, he approaches it this way (1158–12):

> Material things are the shadows of that which is spiritual in its essence. Now you experience that H_2O is water—everywhere! Then water is water, and a part of the whole, with all the essential elements that make for the ability of manifestations in bringing life, in quenching the thirst. And it becomes active thus in *whatever* sphere or phase it finds itself; whether in the frigid, as ice; in the temperate, as water; or in that phase as steam. Yet *everywhere*—in *every phase*—its activities are the same!

Our physical bodies are solid matter (ice), our mental and emotional bodies are fluid (liquid), and our soul/spirit bodies are cloud-like (vapor). All three are the same—water in different forms and conditions: solid, liquid, and vapor! The Water of Life is therefore in our bodies, minds, and souls. All are here with us.

In readings 3143-1 and 5657-11, Cayce equates gaseous states with spiritual conditions and realms, noting that we came out of the gaseous condition (vapor) into matter (solid) and are now moving out of matter toward the more ethereal, vaporous, gaseous condition of spirit and soul.

How do we become more conscious of the Spirit's, the Holy Spirit's, presence within us, within our little spirits? Cayce gives us the answer, a difficult answer. We may, on occasion, perceive the Spirit through our five physical senses, but the better way and therefore the one we must strive for is through "spiritual intuitive forces": "It partakes of the spiritual intuitive forces as comes from close communion with the Holy Spirit, the promised Comforter, the consciousness of the Christ." (262-15)

We need to budget time in our lives for this communion. From such communions come the all-important "spiritual intuitive forces." But this won't work if we simply attempt to *talk to* the Holy Spirit from our outer, conscious mind. We must learn to listen, I prefer *feel*, from our deep inner mind and heart, the Holy Spirit's message. That is where true communion occurs.

Here it is important to understand that Cayce taught that "Christ is not a man." (991-1) Jesus is the man and Christ is the Spirit. The Christ Spirit was *within* Jesus, and even Jesus credited his gifts and wisdom to this Spirit in John 14 and 15.

God's spirit with us is the *Emmanuel* (literally, "God with us") of the ancient prophecies. According to these prophecies, a *messiah* (literally, "anointed one") was to be sent from God into the earth to awaken and bring salvation and resurrection to all souls. The disciple John begins his gospel with a poetic vision into the role and influence of this messiah. It begins, "In the beginning was the Word . . . ." Actually, in the original Greek, this text reads, "In the beginning was the Logos . . . ." *Logos* means much more than the English term *word*. It means the divine, rational principle that governs and develops the universe. There is an incident in John's gospel in which Jesus actually uses two Greek words for *word*, giving emphasis to the greater meaning behind *logos*. Jesus was in an argument with the Pharisees and scribes of the Temple and had made the famous statement, "Before Abraham was, I am." (8:58). Of course, he is speaking from the perspective of the Logos, through which all was made and to which Jesus is attuned. Here is that statement (8:43): "Why do you not understand my word [*lalian*]? It is because you cannot hear my word [*logon*, a form of *logos*]." It is clear that Jesus is drawing a distinction between words that are in speech and the source of all expression, truth, and understanding, the Logos. Also, in the original Greek text, there is no masculine pronoun in the initial sentences of the passage; therefore the text actually reads:

"In the beginning was the Logos, and the Logos was with God, and the Logos was God. This One was in the beginning with God. All things were made through this One. Without this One was not anything made that has been made. In this One was life; and the life was the light of humanity. And the light shines in the darkness; and the darkness does not apprehend it. There came a man, sent from God, whose name was John [the Baptist]. The same came as a witness, that he might bear witness to the light, that all might believe through him. He was not the light, but came that he might bear witness to the light. This was the true light, even the light that lights every person coming into the world. This One was in the world, and the world was made through this One, and the world knew him not. This One came to his own, and they that were his own did not receive him. But as many as received him, to them gave he the right to become children of God, even to them that believe on his name: who were not born of blood, nor of the will of the flesh, nor of the will of man, but of God. And the Logos became flesh, and dwelt among us; and we beheld its glory, glory as of the only begotten from the Father, full of grace and truth."

This is such an inspired opening to the most mystical of the four gospels. But another gem behind this new understanding of "the Word" is in chapter 8:31. Here Jesus informs us that *we* can abide in the Logos, and thereby receive the truth directly and be made free: "If you abide in my Logos, then you are truly disciples of mine; and you shall know the truth, and the truth shall make you free."

According to many religions, especially ancient Hinduism, the Maker put a little of Him/Herself in each us during the initial creation. This means that at a deep level, we are gods within God, little "I ams" within the great I AM. In this way, Jesus, at a deeper level, was also the "Son of God" and we are sons and daughters of God. As Jesus stated by quoting Psalm 62, "You are gods." Like Jesus, we are both sons and daughters of "man" while, at the same time, sons and daughters of God. The human and the divine abide together in us. The great challenge is to integrate these two in the proper order. At present, most of us are humans who love spirituality. The goal is to become Spirits, Godly Spirits, who are temporarily manifesting in human form and consciousness. After the resurrection, Jesus withdrew into oneness with the Maker, but he said that we are channels of the Maker's light and love into this world until he returns to lead a Golden Age.

As Cayce has said in several readings, the flow of life and wisdom begins in the *Spirit*, flows into the *mental*, and then makes its presence visible in the *physical*—not the other way around, as we too often believe. Let's first get in touch with the Spirit, through the Mind, and then our physical lives will change for the better and we'll be able to do more good than if we did so on our own without the Spirit.

Cayce makes this clear statement: "The Spirit is the true life." (262-29)

When we look around, we see multiplicity, diversity, and separateness. You are *there*. I am *here*. Your thoughts are *yours*; mine are *mine*. Oneness is not evident. Yet, from Edgar Cayce's trance-like connection to the Universal Consciousness, he saw and taught oneness: "The first lesson . . . should be *One*—One—One—*One*; Oneness of God, oneness of man's relations, oneness of force, oneness of time, oneness of purpose, *Oneness* in every effort—Oneness—Oneness!" (900-429) For Cayce, our thoughts are not just ours! In fact, he could tell exactly what others had been thinking, because thoughts leave an impression upon the Universal Consciousness. Cayce could "read" these impressions. Thoughts, for him, were "deeds." When giving a reading for an individual, Cayce had difficulty determining if he or she had actually manifested a particular behavior or just thought about it, because thoughts make as strong an impression on the Collective Consciousness as actions! That's a scary thought—oops, I just made another impression on the Collective Consciousness! Cayce was concerned that we all grasp the implications of this unavoidable oneness.

Is it possible that everyone and everything is a part of some unseen Collective, some indivisible Whole, within which all multiplicity exists, and each affects the composition of this Collective? Cayce says yes: "Not only God is God, but self is a part of that oneness." (900–181) In several readings, Cayce pressed us to simply believe this and live as if it were true! In this way we would come to know that it is indeed true. "Let this, my children, be the lesson for you: The intent in relating to each and every individual should be to bring forth that best element in each, in *Oneness* of purpose, in oneness of spirit, in oneness of mind, towards each and every one that you contact—for the individuals, in the final analysis, are one." (288–19) In some manner that we don't readily perceive, you and I—and all the individuals we meet and interact with each day—are one.

These are hard teachings to understand and harder to live by. We've all heard the admonition *think before you speak*, but this level of oneness would suggest that we should *think* before we think. Does thinking negative thoughts about another person actually affect that person at some unseen level? Do these negative thoughts make a recording upon a Collective Consciousness, a recording that someone like Cayce can read? Ancient Hinduism included the concept of an *Akasha*, an etheric film that records all thoughts, all words, and all actions from the first Om of creation until the last Om of silence. Nothing is lost. Nothing is forgotten. Nothing is unknowable. Watching Cayce give readings on the activities of celestial godlings who lived before the Earth even existed certainly suggests that nothing is forgotten or lost or unknowable. While his body was on the couch and his conscious mind was for all intents and purposes asleep, his deeper mind could tell us about a long-forgotten event in one's early childhood that still had its effect on the present, or an ancient past life that influenced the outer self's feelings in the present life. In some readings for individuals, he would mention the house they lived in and what they were doing as the reading was about to begin, such as: "Yes, we have the red mail box. We are entering the house. She is in the bedroom praying."

In the 1960s and '70s, when meditation was taking hold in this country, meditators began to speak of experiencing a sense of oneness with all of life when they reached deeper levels in their meditation. When questioned about this, all they could say was that, at some moment in their meditation, all life seemed connected. But the gap between this inner meditative feeling and our outer-sensory perception is a chasm. There is simply no outer-sensory corroboration for such a position. Oneness is an inner perception that defies outer evidence. Apparently, oneness has to be experienced firsthand in order to overcome all the outer contradictions to its existence. And short of rare miraculous epiphanies, meditation appears to be the best way to perceive the unseen oneness. Even Jesus had trouble making the oneness argument with his disciple Philip at the Last Supper, finally conceding that if he could not believe Jesus' oneness with the Father and that Philip had therefore known the Father by knowing Jesus, then let the outer miracles act as evidence of this oneness with God.

But let's press this oneness idea a little further. How can selfish or evil people still be in oneness with the Collective? And if they are, simply because there is no way to be outside of the Whole, then why are they allowed to do so much harm to others in the Collective? In a very complex discussion between one of the greatest questioners of Edgar Cayce, Morton Blumenthal, #900, and the "sleeping" Edgar Cayce, attuned to the Collective, we can find some insights into these hard questions. Since the discussion is so complex, I'll paraphrase here:

Morton: On Oct. 15, Thursday, at home I had this dream: It seemed my mother and I were in a hotel where many people were passing by. Then there was a typewriter with a sheet of blank paper in it, waiting to be used by one of the many applicants for the position of stenographer. The typewriter also seemed to be waiting for my more perfect understanding of something else—some final thing—the first three principles of which I had two. In the midst of all of this, a voice said: '*All* of these are *God!*'

Cayce: This dream is presenting to the entity the oneness of purpose, of intent, of the *whole being as one*. For *all* is of God, see? And as the entity gains knowledge from living the various phases of oneness, he gains that first principle of which the other two he already has. That first principle is this: God is in you, manifesting to other individuals through every phenomenized situation that is presented in a physical world. For, every force which may not be separated or produced by man is of God and of the Universal Forces. These are the three forces in man: (1) Spiritual—of God; (2) Cosmic—the forces made by man; and (3) Subconscious—the force that bridges the Spiritual and the Cosmic, connecting the spiritual with the cosmic.

Morton: It seems to me that this dream imagery tries again and again to drive home to my dense physical mind that God is One . . .

Cayce: (Interrupting) Correct.

Morton: God is all of these people passing in the hotel and all of the applicants for the stenographer job . . .

Cayce: (Interrupting) Correct.

Morton: All these people are phenomenized forms of God. Also God is all of these consciousnesses . . .

Cayce: (Interrupting) Except that God is not the cosmic forces made by free-will man. These are not related to spiritual forces. These are earth made.

(Based on 900–147)

In many of his readings, Cayce explained that evil is man's misuse of the gift of free will. The Creator allows this because free will is the only way for any soul to reach its original purpose for existence: to know itself to be itself yet *choose* to be one with the Whole, with the Creator and the creation. If free will is taken away, then the soul no longer has the potential to become an eternal companion with its creator. As the theological concept goes, man was made a little less than the angels but with the potential to judge even the angels. This is why souls misusing free will are allowed more time to discover their true purpose, even if they do much harm along the way. Eventually, as recorded in the Revelation, God will stop time and separate misusers from those who have tried to fulfill their purpose. He/She will then "wipe the tears from everyone's eyes" and set up "a new heaven and a new earth" for the companionable souls to enjoy with God.

According to Cayce's readings and many other classic sources, before anything was created there existed something that caused the creation to begin. The potential for the creation—what Cayce often referred to as "the first impulse, the first cause"—was latent in pre-creation emptiness. A good way for us to grasp how there could be anything *before* the creation is to think of the infinite emptiness as a consciousness, much like our own, except that this consciousness was infinite and perfectly still; no thoughts; quiet. Imagining this with our own minds is one of the states of meditation: a clear, quiet mind—hard to do for even a few minutes. At some moment, this infinite mind began to move, to conceive, and the creation began. Imagine how the idea of light awoke, and playing with this idea, the infinite mind conceived of stars and galaxies of all shapes, sizes, and colors. At some moment in this conception process, Cayce says, the Universal Consciousness conceived of companions to itself, companions made in its own image: minds, with life, creativity, and free will. Countless little minds were conceived in the one, infinite mind.

At first, we all remained consciously connected to the One Mind. But as we began to use our free wills to experience individual consciousness, we focused more on our own consciousness and gradually lost our connection with the Infinite Mind. We did not go anywhere. There was nowhere to go beyond the Whole. We simply lost consistent consciousness of our oneness with the Infinite Consciousness. Today, billions of years after it all began, we struggle to regain and retain conscious awareness of the One Mind within which we all exist and with which we are all destined to consciously companion forever—if we choose to.

Just as this is all getting clearer, Cayce tosses a brick into our thinking when he says such mind-boggling things as "there is no time, no space." He explains that at a deep level, there actually is no beginning, no end; all time is one. He explains that there actually is no *here* and no *there*. As demonstrated by his own readings, he could tell someone what he or she (the deeper self) thought eons ago, as if it were yesterday, and could physically be in Virginia Beach while viewing a person in San Diego! During his readings, there was indeed no time, no space. All was one.

Cayce said it this way: "Learn these lessons well: First, the continuity of life. There is no time; it is one time. There is no space; it is one space. There is no force, other than all force in its various phases and applications. The individual is such a part of God that one's thoughts may become crimes or miracles, for thoughts are deeds. That that one metes must be met again. That one applies will be applied again and again until that oneness of time, space, force are learned and the individual is one with the whole." (4341-1)

Fortunately for our three-dimensional selves, he did instruct that time and space are helpful tools for developing souls to use in our day-to-day, step-by-step process of application and enlightenment. But his deeper mind did not want us to get lost in the limitations of time and space, encouraging us to budget some time and space for experiencing the timelessness and spacelessness; in other words, the oneness. He also instructed seekers to "watch the self go by"—watch the self interact with others, watch one's mind thinking about situations and people—and see if one's words, actions, and thoughts reflect the truth of the oneness or the illusion of separateness, multiplicity, and diversity.

From Cayce's trance perspective, the greatest evil in the earth and in the hearts and minds of individuals is contention, faultfinding, lovers of self, and lovers of praise, because these forces separate. The greatest good in the world is love, patience, kindness, forgiveness, and under-standing, because these forces unite, for "these are times when every effort should be made to preserve the universality of love." (877-29) He instructed one person to "study the truths about oneness, whether Jewish, Gentile, Greek, or heathen!" (136-12) Among religions, Cayce said that wherever the principle of one God and one people is taught, there is truth. And that in many of the world's great religions, the principle of oneness is there, but men have "turned this aside to meet their own immediate needs, as a moralist or the head of any independent power, but 'Know the Lord thy God is One!' whether this is directing one of the Confucius thought, Brahman thought, Buddha thought, Mohammedan thought . . . there is *only* one. The whole law and gospel of every age has said, 'There is *one* God!'" (364-9)

As with all of these concepts, they begin within our individual minds and hearts, and since there is oneness, the more individuals believe in the oneness and live it in their lives, the more it makes an impression upon the Collective Consciousness and finds its way into other individual minds and hearts. We are the leaven that can leaven the whole loaf of humanity. Let's budget time to experience the oneness in meditation. Let's practice oneness in our thoughts about others and interactions with others. Ultimately, despite all the indications to the contrary, the world and humanity will be one.

5

Mind Is the Builder

*F*rom his deep attunement to the Mind of God, that "Universal Consciousness," Edgar Cayce stated that mind is the light, the builder, and the bridge to liberation and enlightenment. Here are some of his perspectives on the mind:

> The Spirit moved . . . and there was Light—Mind. The Light became the light of men.   1947-3

> In the beginning God created the heavens and the earth. How? The Mind of God moved, and matter, form, came into being. Mind, then, in God the Father, is the builder. How much more, then, would or should Mind be the builder in the experience of those that have put on Christ or God, in Him, in His coming into the earth?"
> 262-78

> Each entity finds itself in a three-dimensional phase of existence or experience: the world without, the world within, and the mind that may span or bridge the two.   1100-26

Mind is the light, the builder, and the bridge between spirit and body. Cayce explained that life, all life, begins in the *spirit*, which is the creative force that brings all into existence. Then *mind* takes this life essence and builds with it. Finally, the *physical* is the result: "Mind the builder, the spirit the creator, the material [is] that created. Great truth! Keep it before you." (900–374) It certainly is a powerful concept to keep before us. All outer "things" have their origin in the unseen spiritual forces, then find expression in the mind, and ultimately appear out here in the physical. Cayce frequently asked us to accept that "the unseen forces are greater than the seen." If we want to change something, it must begin in the spirit and the mind.

"That you think, that you put your Mind to work upon, to live upon, to feed upon, to live with, to abide with, to associate with in the mind, *that* your soul-body becomes! That is the law. That is the destiny." He expands upon this: "Mind [is] the builder, the appreciater, the paralleler, the drawing of conclusions, the chooser . . . " (1100–26) And, Cayce says, mind is driven by "the ideal."

The Ideal Is the Mind's Navigator

"As you contemplate, as you meditate, as you look upon the Mind, know the Mind has many windows. And as you look out of your inner self, know where you are looking, [where] you are seeking. What is your ideal? What would you have your mind-body to become?" (262–78; also see "The Ideal" section in chapter 32)

In a deep contemplation session on this teaching, my deeper mind saw the ancient boat of pharaoh, with its twenty-four oarsmen and the navigator's hut on the bow. As I sought to know the meaning of this imagery, Cayce's teaching about the twelve elders before the Throne of God in the book of the Revelation came to mind. He said that they represent the twelve paired cranial nerves (twenty-four) in our own heads! As these nerves turn their attention away from worldly pursuits and toward heavenly ones, they bring a "new heaven and a new earth," meaning a new mind, a new body. As I reflected on this, I realized that the twenty-four oarsmen on pharaoh's boat represented these same nerves and their ability to bring us across the barrier, which the Nile represented, between what the Egyptians called "the land of the living," which is the place of the physically incarnate, and "the land of the dead," the realm of the spiritually living. I realized that the navigator was indeed the ideal held as we sought to cross the barrier between this world and the spiritual.

"That upon which it [the mind] feeds it becomes. The most important experience of this or any individual entity is to first know what is the ideal—spiritually. Who and what is your pattern?" (357-13) Cayce frequently said that Christ is the consciousness, and Jesus is the pattern. Jesus, for Cayce, is the ideal pattern to use to build one's own mind—just as one would use a pattern to make clothes from new fabric. Jesus exemplified a human at one with God and making that oneness manifest in his life among others. Cayce often noted that Jesus simply went around doing good according to God's inner guidance to Him—an ideal for all of us.

Consider this from Cayce: "What, then, is an ideal? As concerning your fellow man, He gave, 'As you would that others do to you, do you even so to them'; take no thought, worry not, be not overanxious about the body. For He knows what you have need of. In the place you are, in the consciousness in which you find yourself, is that which is needed today, now, for your greater, your better, your more wonderful unfoldment. This is that attitude of mind that puts away hate, malice, anxiety, and jealousy. And it creates in their stead the fruits of the spirit: love, patience, mercy, longsuffering, kindness, gentleness. Against these there is no law. They break down barriers; they bring peace and harmony; they bring the outlook upon life of not finding fault because someone 'forgot', someone's judgment was bad, someone was selfish today. These you can overlook, for so did He." (357-13)

Such a state of attitude, of mind, toward life sets up a powerful map for navigating oneself through the day's challenges and opportunities. This is an ideal, a navigational star by which to guide one each day. With this ideal, the mind approaches every obstacle, every crosscurrent, every undertow, and wends its way through them by holding to the ideal. This is the power of an ideal. Yet, as we grow and learn, we may see the need to adjust our ideal. Cayce encouraged us to write our ideals down, but to do so in pencil. As we gain a greater understanding, we gain an increasingly better perspective and we adjust our ideal accordingly.

Thoughts Are Deeds

Another fundamental Cayce teaching is this: "Thoughts are deeds, and as their currents run they become miracles or crimes in the experiences of individual life." (281-3) For the deeply attuned Cayce, thoughts were as real as actions. Our thoughts are recorded on the Akashic Record. Remember, Cayce had to strain to determine whether the person he was reading for had actually *done* something or had just *thought* about doing it! "Thoughts are things; just as the Mind is as concrete as a post or tree." (1581-1) The first time I read this, it pained me to think how many times my thoughts had done harm to another and placed a negative influence in the Collective Mind. Watching our thoughts is important.

Watch Self Pass By

Cayce was once asked: "How may I learn to know self as I am known?" He answered: "Being able to literally stand aside and watch self pass by! Take the time to occasionally be sufficiently introspective of that, that may happen in self's relation to others, to see the reactions of others as to that as was done by self; for no man lives to himself, no man dies to himself . . . Being able, then, to see self as others see you . . . Stand aside and watch self pass by!" (262-9) This is a powerful learning tool.

For Cayce, this was not just good mental advice, it was good physical advice: "If the body will watch self and the reactions of the various foods or preparations, and draw a comparison from what may be termed a combination of all the various authorities, then the body will find what is best for self. See?" (278-2) Want to know the best diet for yourself? Watch how the various foods and cooking methods affect you. This will be better advice than anyone else can give you, because your own body reveals it.

The Subliminal Mind

Dreams and meditations are two of Cayce's most recommended means for fully engaging the power of the mind. According to Cayce, our subliminal mind will engage with our outer mind to review and discuss all influences: "In this there is seen both the action of the sub-conscious and subliminal mind and the physical mind, reasoning to-gether, as it were, of the past, present, and future conditions as relating to the mental attitude of the entity; for, as is seen in the final analysis of the real Mind, the Builder, and as this is presented in the view of the dreams, the meditations of the entity in those days when the inner consciousness of the entity built in the mental forces those condi-tions as would bring the great joy, peace, and happiness to the entity, these, as we see, took on physical forms in the mental aspirations of the entity." (900-205)

As we seek within ourselves through dreams, meditations, and deep reflections, our subliminal mind will convey the insights.

Subconscious: The Police

The only real guide that may be relied upon is that subconscious force that is as the police to the entity, both in the physical, mate-rial, and in the spiritual planes. And, as this [the subconscious] will guide and direct the entity, in that same way and manner as the police in their regular capacity . . . in the physical life. [What a fasci-nating concept. Our subconscious is our conscience, our policing power.] That is, the police, the subconscious mind, represent the law that guides, directs, and that way upon which the entity, which any entity, may rely for the enforcement of that which will keep in peace, in war, in any condition, that straight way for the best inter-est of each and every individual.   900-243

However, even as physical police departments can become corrupt, so can our subconscious police become misdirected by powerful sug-gestions of self-doubt, self-condemnation. "In the same way and man-ner as these (the police) may become subject to all of the vicissitudes that are ever present within the conditions in life, so may the subcon-scious forces, mis-directed, mis-guided, or seeking to belittle the self . . . through its experience in the earth's plane." (900-243) The only way to protect against this misdirection is to hold to a higher ideal that lifts us beyond our self-doubt, self-condemnation. God does not condemn us; God has erected no barrier. Self is the only obstacle to full enlightenment and reunion.

Levels of Consciousness

Cayce identifies three levels of consciousness, or dimensions, of mind: conscious, subconscious, and superconscious.

Conscious mind is the level that we are most familiar with. It is the level within which our personality and three-dimensional self develops and has much of its activity.

The subconscious is that part of our minds that bridges the outer self with the spiritual self. According to Cayce, the subconscious is both in the body, through the autonomic system, and beyond the body, in the soul realms of telepathy, non-physical life, and timelessness. This mind is the mind of the soul. As the mind of our outer self is the conscious mind and that portion containing our personality, so the subconscious mind contains our developing "individuality," which Cayce identifies as our true self.

The superconscious level is the portion made in the image of the Creator, as recorded in Genesis. It is that portion of us that is a god, or *godling*, as the ancient Egyptians termed it. Cayce explained that the superconscious is a thing apart from anything earthly and only makes its presence known or is knowable when the soul-self lifts itself and portions of the conscious mind up into the vast, expansive level that is the superconscious. This is the portion of our being that Cayce referred to when he said, "Not only God is God, but self is a part of that oneness."

To know the superconscious, Cayce says that one must learn to achieve deep levels of meditation. And if a dream feels more like a vision than a dream, then it most likely originated from this highest level of consciousness.

At death, the conscious mind is gradually absorbed into the subconscious (the mind of the surviving soul), and the subconscious becomes the operative mind, with the superconscious now in the position the subconscious held while incarnate. Later, upon reincarnation, the subconscious projects another portion of itself into the newly developing outer, three-dimensional mind. Intuitions, "knowings," and psychic perceptions come from the projected subconscious. Cayce explains that not the entire subconscious is projected; some of it remains in very high levels of perception and activity. But the portion that is in the body maintains the autonomic systems of the body (respiration, circulation, digestion, etc.) and the seven spiritual centers, or chakras, which correspond with the seven endocrine glands.

Mind is our true nature. It is that portion of ourselves that lives forever. What would it be like to live our lives as minds in bodies, rather than bodies with minds? Surprisingly, Cayce considered the mind to be a savior, a redeemer. It is that portion of our being that can mend and restore us. Let's engage our minds and fully awaken to our spiritual selves.

6

Matter, Mind, and Spirit

*W*ere there really ancient gods that mingled with humans as the myths of most cultures record? If so, where are these gods today? Amazingly, the Cayce readings and modern depth–psychologists have some possible answers. Take, for example, a reading for a woman (1554–3) in which Cayce implies that the ancient Greek gods were actually "mental forces." He explains to the woman that in that incarnation she struggled against the urges for material gratification by using aid from the gods of the mental forces. This experience gave her powerful reasoning abilities in this present incarnation, abilities to use her mind to overcome the power of matter and material ideals.

To a young man, in reading 442–5, Cayce warns that he has so lost touch with his soul–mind that matter overcomes mind, making it difficult for him to get fully healthy. Cayce went on to tell this man that he must awaken his mind to these higher concepts and ideals in order to overcome these influences. The "gods" of his mental forces were blocked from conveying their powers upon him by his complete acceptance of the powers of materiality.

To a woman, in reading 1152–5, Cayce gave what may be his most inspired insight into the power of the mind over matter and the role *spirit* plays in the *quickening* necessary for health and enlightenment:

It is true that the body mentally, the body physically, should be and is capable of resuscitating and revitalizing itself, if it is raised in a *spiritual* direction. Hence mind over matter is not to be lightly spoken of, nor is there any disparaging remark to be made as to the body-physical being revivified, resuscitated, spiritualized such that there is no reaction that may not be revivified.

He then says that "any application of any influence in man's condition . . . that arouses the nature of . . . man's consciousness to the *awareness* of the God-consciousness to make it a whole" will lift us to a level of consciousness in which God's Spirit can do its part in our healing and enlightenment. Cayce explains that we have an important role in this *co-creative* process:

To man hath He [God] given the ministry of those influences within the material world, where ministry may be made to the needs temporal, the needs mental, the needs spiritual. The ministerations *must* answer, to be sure, to the *divine within;* else they cannot, they do not *quicken.* For God alone quickens into life that which has through any form of error misdirected its flow through even the physical body. Man may minister, man may direct—only the Father, God, can give, *does* give the increase—the *quickening.* For it is true indeed, "My Spirit," saith the Father, "beareth witness with thy spirit that ye *are* the children of the *living* Father."   1152-5

As Jesus explained to the woman at the well, God is Spirit. Our minds must change, must reach to the higher levels of the gods of the mental forces that overcome all the seemingly powerful limitations of the physical, material self and this world. The real healing, the real enlightenment comes when our *elevated* minds open to the quickening power of the Spirit and the Spirit flows into and through us so completely as to revivify, rejuvenate, and make whole our body, mind, and soul.

Then enter into that quietude in prayer and in supplication for that *strength* to now manifest those truths as are being, and as have been, gained by the entity, and the entity will find that he does *not*

meet these alone, but with that guiding hand of the Spirit that gives
to the entity the power, the force, the words, necessary to bring
the condition of chaos unto that quietude, even as was said of
Him, "Even the winds and the waves obey His Voice."   900-176

The physical organism is constructed in such a way and manner
that if the balance is kept in the diet, in the normal activity, and the
mental forces replenished, then the body should readjust itself,
refacilitate itself; making for not only resuscitation and revivifying of
the necessary influences but carrying on and reproducing itself.

1040-1

The body should in its elements be able, as it does continually, to
reproduce itself; making for not only revivifying or resuscitating
forces but keeping nominally alive.   1038-1

Notice his use of the word *nominal*. In Cayce's vision, life is much
more than living healthfully. He often said, "It is not all of life to live,
nor all of death to die." Life must be lived for something, not just lived.
Even when life is healthy, it is simply "nominal" until it has a purpose.

In most cases, the Cayce discourses were generated by a question
and answer format, as we see in this next dialogue:

Q: Is it possible for our bodies to be rejuvenated in this incarnation?
A: Possible. The body is an atomic structure, the units of energy
around which there are the movements of atomic forces that are
ever the pattern of a universe. Then, when these atoms are made to
conform or rely upon or to be one with the spiritual import, the
spiritual activity, then they revivify, then they make for constructive
forces.   262-85

Being "one with the spiritual import" is key to Cayce's method toward revivifying and making for constructive forces. This is a difficult
concept for most of us to understand. As we continue, I believe we'll
understand further.

> If there will be gained that consciousness, there need not be ever the necessity of a physical organism aging . . . seeing this, feeling this, knowing this, ye will find that not only does the body become revivified, but by creating in every atom of its being the knowledge of the activity of this Creative Force . . . spirit, mind, body [are] renewed.
>
> 1299-1

Notice his phrasing, "that consciousness" which will ultimately lead to no aging. What is that consciousness that he is referring to? Look at this next statement (my bold type):

> In the present there may be gained within self the raising within self **that consciousness** of the at-onement with the spiritual forces that may revivify, regenerate, arouse that of health and happiness even under adverse conditions in materiality.
>
> 618-3

There is a state of consciousness that can heal. This consciousness is at–one with the spiritual forces. Cayce includes spiritual powers with mental and physical powers.

Notice this next comment, which seems to be referring to an un-known sequence that leads to full, healthy life through some mystical path of transcendence.

> How is the way shown by the Master? What is the promise in Him? The last to be overcome is death. Death of what? The soul cannot die, for it is of God. The body may be revivified, rejuvenated—and it is to that end it may, the body, *transcend* the earth and its influences.
>
> 262-85

Cayce once noted that you cannot cure a quinine mind of malaria with anything but quinine! Nevertheless, it is not the quinine that is the healer but the mind within the person that believes the quinine will heal. The source of healing is within us. If we realize this and begin to take hold of our inner thoughts, beliefs, and consciousness, then we can make significant changes in our outer condition.

We've already seen the first of the next two excerpts, but let's look at it again, this time with the emphasis on "within."

> In the present there may be gained within self the raising **within** self
> that consciousness of the at-onement with the spiritual forces that
> may revivify, regenerate, arouse that of health and happiness even
> under adverse conditions in materiality.   618-3

> The revivifying forces are the *natural* sources of energies through
> quietness **within** any given activity that makes for strengthening for
> resistances of every nature in a physical body.   587-5

   In this next discourse, you'll notice a reference to "thine inner self."
When I first came across it, I was curious about this other self that I was
not familiar with, especially since Cayce frequently indicated that it was
quite distinct from my outer self. Then, one day while waking from a
dream, I had an experience that helped me sense the difference between my outer and inner self. I was dreaming. I knew I was dreaming,
and I was enjoying the dream and thinking about how I would record
it in my dream journal when I finally awoke. When I did fully wake up,
I remembered the dream and my desire to record it, but I decided to
first go to the bathroom and empty my bladder. When I returned, I had
absolutely no recall of the dream. Nothing! I couldn't believe it. There
was no dream content in my mind. Therefore, I lay back down on the
bed and began to go back into sleep when suddenly there was the
dream content. In my desire to understand this, I practiced moving
from the dream state out into the conscious state to see if I could better
bridge these two realities. It became clear to me that when I was in the
dream, I really felt like "I" was conscious and dreaming. However, when
I was out in the conscious state, I also felt that "I" was conscious, but
without any dream content. The more I played with this movement
between the two realities, the more I realized that there truly were two,
clearly discernible parts to my being. One was aligned with my subconscious mind, and experienced and possessed the dream content. And
the other was aligned with my conscious mind and physical world and
contained no dream, unless I gradually awoke and purposefully conveyed the content over to it. Even then, it could barely hold on to it for

any length of time! Despite these distinct parts, I felt that I was really me when I was in either. "I" was dreaming, and "I" was emptying my bladder. My inner and outer self were familiar to me, but not to each other. The veil between them was so opaque that I could not see back into the subconscious once I was fully in the outer consciousness. But the movement between the two was so subtle that I didn't even notice I had moved out of one and into the other.

In this next discourse, we have Cayce referring to the work, or role, our inner self plays in the healing process, and the help it needs.

> The revivifying influences will give thine inner self that which will create, that which will build in the body, as thou holdest to that thou knowest within thine self—that He, the Giver of all good and perfect gifts, is renewing thy strength and thy life within thee; and that thou wilt *use* same in His service so long as the days are given unto thee for thy activities in this material world. And we will find *strength* being built in thine body as the stamina of steel! And, as the vital forces renew thy vitality in thine body, *use* thy mental self.
>
> 716-2

If we also remember that the subconscious mind (the mind of the inner self) is amenable to suggestion, then many of Cayce's guidelines about positive belief and active mindfulness make real sense.

Coordinating body–mind–spirit and taking hold of the forces within us will lead us to health and rejuvenation. However, for Cayce, the answer to why we want to be healthy and rejuvenated is as important as how we achieve it.

Two people can do exactly the same things toward rejuvenation and wellness but get different results. So often, the influencing force in these cases is their attitude. One is hopeful and expectant, the other doubts or feels unworthy. Attitude is a powerful, unseen influence in the outcome of any activity.

> To be sure, there should be rather that expectant attitude of the body . . . for unless there is the expectancy, unless there is hope, the mind's outlook becomes a drag, a drug on one that is being

attacked from within by the various diseases of a physical body.

572-5

Cayce often hyphenated the word *disease* in an effort to convey the real source of disease as being a dis-ease in the system, physically and mentally. When a being is at ease with itself, health is usually present. But health cannot be maintained long when something within a person is uneasy, or at *dis*-ease. Notice also that Cayce continues to emphasize the importance of the right mental attitude: being hopeful and expectant.

Doubt was also on Cayce's list of don'ts, as we see in this next instruction:

> *Do not* become morose. Do not doubt the abilities of those influences in the spiritual life to meet the needs of the body physically, mentally, spiritually, and we will revivify these things.   458-2

> Nothing save self stands in the way of the entity *making* or becoming a channel of blessings to many! For the entity may be assured, for the entity will find, nothing in heaven or hell or earth may separate thee from the knowledge and the use of the *I AM Presence* within, save selfishness—or self!   440-20

This is a hard one to accept. Few of us take full responsibility for our circumstances in life and in health. But it sure appears that Cayce is listing "self" as the only limitation to success.

This next Cayce comment reminds me of my parents' admonitions to "pull yourself together" or "get hold of yourself." Mind over circumstances, whether they are physical, emotional, or mental, is a powerful tool toward changing the prevailing condition. Here Cayce reminds us, in this excerpt from a previously mentioned reading, that we shouldn't use discouraging remarks when we or others are struggling to overcome a condition.

> Hence mind over matter is not to be lightly spoken of, nor is there

any disparaging remark to be made as to the ability of the body-
physical to be revivified, resuscitated, spiritualized such that there
is no reaction that may not be revivified.   1152-5

The Cayce records are filled with the admonition to "live what you
know to be true and right." Our actions must reflect our deepest beliefs
and values. If they do, then the Life Force can flow through us without
getting meshed in a web of hypocrisy, contradiction, and disharmony.
Cayce often identified incoordination of the two nervous systems as
one of the major causes of illness, equating it with the two parts of
ourselves (inner and outer) being at war with one another. Here he calls
for us to hold to a simple truth:

For *He* hath shown the way—not by some mysterious fluid, not by
some unusual vibration, but by the simple method of *living* that
which is *life* itself. *Think* no evil; *hear* no evil. And as the Truth flows
as a stream of life through the Mind in all its phases or aspects, and
purifies same, so will it purify and revivify and rejuvenate the body.
For once this effacement urge is overcome, then may there begin
the rejuvenation.   294-183

In this case, and with many of us today, we actually seem to get in a
self-destructive mode, or as Cayce said, an "effacement urge." Who can
save us from ourselves? All the outer applications can't overcome the
desires of the ruler of the house. First, one must stop effacing oneself or
destroying oneself, for whatever reason we may think justified. Then,
self can be transformed.

Mind *is* the master.   2529-1

Paradoxically, this powerful statement is frequently offset by a "nevertheless" statement, such as this one: "Yet, physical conditions need the
[therapeutic] activity that may regenerate or revivify the abilities for
reproduction of self through the afflicted or disturbed areas of the body."
(2529-1)
One can only conclude that the mind is the master, yet we also need

therapeutic applications to help along the regenerative process.

> It may appear long, but—keep that attitude of being the channel
> through which more love of the divine nature may be given, even
> as ye would be *shown* that towards the ways and manners for the
> helpfulness in the material physical body.   1199-3

Cayce often encouraged those who were in the worst situations to
get out of their self-absorption with their problems by simply looking
around for someone else who needed help, and helping them—with no
thought of reward. Something in the spirit of helpfulness has a magical
effect upon the helper.

In this next case, we see someone who is suppressing herself, either
from guilt, self-consciousness, anxiety, or fear. Since every living thing
has an inner drive to express life, suppression is against the flow of life
and must therefore be transformed in order for life to flow and health
to return. He encourages her to get interested in something, as well as
to keep up with the therapy.

> The destruction of the blood forces [is] by *suppression* of self in a
> mental manner. Hence, the necessity of directing and interesting
> self in a *fad*, or even a *fancy*, and keeping self interested in same, as
> well as correcting the physical conditions.   5554-2

As we have seen, the mind and the mental attitude play major roles
in the healing and health maintenance process.

Finally, Cayce gives the best attitude to hold for maintaining youth
and youthful influences:

> Let age only ripen thee. For one is ever as young as the heart and
> the purpose. Keep sweet. Keep friendly. Keep Loving, if ye would
> keep young.   3420-1

Unique to Cayce's vision is the idea that seekers of healing and health
must *attune* themselves to the Divine within every cell of their bodies in
order to fully realize the perfected condition. It's like a pattern, a code,

and a vibration that possesses life in its *ideal* condition. It is continual and healthy. When we attune to it, we begin to imbue ourselves with this perfected life pattern or state of being.

> It will require that there be such an attitude in mind, in purpose, in hope, and in relationships to others, that each cell of the body may be *attuned to the divine within*. Each cell must become expectant, that there may be the renewing, the revivifying of the relationships that the soul-entity bears to Creative Forces.   3511-1 (my italics)

> Thus there may be a revivifying, a resuscitating, and a creating of an environment such that the body-mind, with its *spiritual* concepts and its *spiritual* understanding, may arouse the whole of the body-forces to their better functionings.   1620-1 (my italics)

> For the body mentally, in its spiritual attributes for the physical self, may hold much in this manner—as the applications are made, os-teopathically, electrically—not for things to be gotten through with, but *see, feel, know* that these are channels and measures **through which the divine may operate** for effective activity in this body!"
> 1299-1 (my bold)

In this next case, we see that some problems are so big, so deep, so painfully possessing that divine help is needed to fully overcome their influence upon the individual.

> The addition of energy-building forces has not removed the hurt, the disappointment. For this has attacked the physical body through the sensory and sympathetic nervous system, causing the reaction. Not that there is any mental disturbance, no. It is rather a hurt, an injury, a disappointment such that there can only come the renewing, the revivifying, by putting the whole trust, faith and re-newed life *in divine hands*.   4037-1 (my italics)

> Being able to raise within the vibrations of individuals to that which is a resuscitating, a revivifying influence and force *through the deep*

meditation (the attunement of self to the higher vibrations in Creative Forces), these are manifested in man through the promises that are coming from Creative Forces or Energy itself!   993-4
(my italics but Cayce's parenthetical comment)

Meditation, especially deep meditation, is one of the most commonly recommended practices in the Edgar Cayce work. For Cayce, meditation was necessary in order for humans to bridge the gap between this world of outer, physical consciousness and the inner world of the subconscious soul and spirit forces. In this particular discourse, he is identifying the deep meditation practice as a means to attuning self "to the higher vibrations in Creative Forces." *Creative Forces* is a Cayce term for those forces many of us associate with God, Nature, and the powers of Life itself—or as he says himself, "Energy itself!" Learning to become outwardly still and quiet while awakening inwardly to the deeper vibrations, especially those with a spiritual quality to them, can result in higher vibes and the flow of energy, resuscitating energy, through our bodies, minds, and souls.

Let's continue looking into attunement, especially attunement to the divine within.

Put hope and trust and faith in the divine within—the revivifying, the rejuvenating of that spirit of life and truth within every atom of the body. This will put to flight all of those things that hinder a body from giving expression of the most hopeful, the most beautiful.
572-5

There are those forces as may be had from the study, the analyzing of those truths presented in the light of *His* ministry—that One who is the way, the truth and the light. The **analyzing** of these, and the **application** of same in the lives of individuals is an individual experience. But the closer, the nearer one **applies** those tenets, those truths, those principles in one's daily experience, the greater is the ability of the mental and spiritual self to revivify the physical activities of any given body.   2074-1 (my bold)

Again, we see Cayce driving hard on the principle of applying ourselves—seeking, studying, analyzing those tenets and principles we know to be of great importance to us, mentally and spiritually. As the great psychologist Carl Jung pointed out, we cannot deny that there is a spiritual component to humans, no matter how illogical it may appear to some of us. Spirit and spiritual truths are important to the overall health of humans, from the most primitive to the most sophisticated.

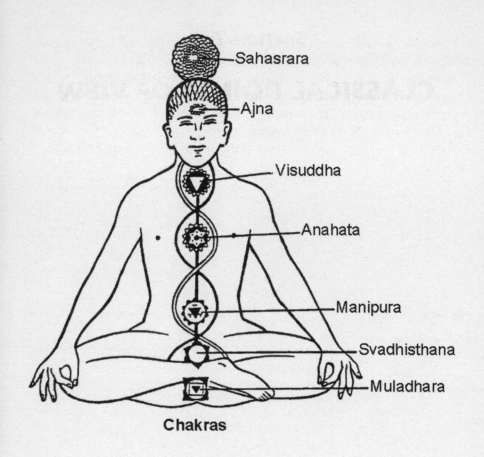

Chakras

Section Two

CLASSICAL POINTS OF VIEW

7

Yoga Sutra

*T*he concept that the human body is designed for both physical and metaphysical experiences goes way back in history some 2,500 years. Perhaps the first text to clearly identify the body as a spiritual device as well as a physical one is Patanjali's *Yoga Sutras*. He wrote that within the human body are pathways and energy zones that may be stimulated in such a manner as to bring about nonphysical activity and higher consciousness. Of course, today many of us are familiar with these pathways and zones: chakras, padmes, sushumna, and ida and pingala (see further elaboration in "Chakras and the Kundalini," chapter 16). Patanjali organized his Yoga Sutras into four parts (padas):

1. Samadhi Pada I: Contemplation and Meditation
2. Sadhana Pada II: The Steps To Union
3. Vibhuti Pada III: Union Achieved And Its Results
4. Kaivalya Pada IV: Illumination and Freedom

Though his original text was written in Sanskrit, making it difficult to translate into modern English, and his writing style is thousands of years old, Patanjali's views are understandable by most modern seekers. I will be using a translation by Swami Venkatesananda, which I've modified according to my own studies and experiences.

Patanjali begins by stating the most fundamental principle of yoga— by *yoga* he means the *unity* that happens when an entity realizes its oneness with the Whole. Here are his own words:

> Yoga [unity] happens when there is stilling [in the sense of con-
> tinual and vigilant watchfulness] of the movement of thought. In the
> light of stillness . . . self is not confused with nor confined to any of
> these. Then [when yoga thus happens], the seer or the homoge-
> neous intelligence which is ignorantly regarded as the separate ex-
> periences of sensations and emotions, and the separate performer
> of actions, is not split up into one or the other of the states or modi-
> fications of the mind, and exists by itself and as itself.

Thus, according to Patanjali, union occurs when an individual perceives that he or she is not simply individual, but universal, one with
the Whole, the All; and this is realized when in the deepest stillness,
when the form–shaping, identity–focused mind is quiet, clear, and yet
alert.

Patanjali goes on to explain the subtleties of union:

> The kindling of the inner psychic fire that at once burns away all the
> impurities and limitations of the mind-stuff, the study both of scrip-
> tural texts and one's own reaction to situations from moment to
> moment, and the meaningful, dynamic and devotional surrender
> to the indwelling *omnipresence*—these three simultaneously con-
> stitute active yoga [union], or practice of the indivisible unity.
>
> When it is clearly understood that the instant realization of cos-
> mic oneness, which is yoga [union], is not the product of any ef-
> fort, how can one "practice" such unity? Surely, active yoga is taught
> not because such practice *results* in the realization of oneness.
> However, it can *aid* in the direction of one's attention *towards* en-
> lightenment, and away from the elements that cause mental tur-
> moil, which, as a result of such turning away, are weakened.
>
> The mind is restless because of the many unresolved problems.
> The elements that disturb mental equilibrium and thus generate
> psychic distress . . . are subtle, and not to be confused with their
> gross expansion as likes and dislikes, habits (good and bad), vanity
> and such personality traits. However, these subtle sources of psy-

chic distress can be dispelled by resolving each in its own cause [or by confronting each of them with its own true opposite].

Now with the fundamentals established and the warnings about how subtle the distracting influences are, Patanjali begins to identify locations within the human body and their metaphysical influence upon the process toward unity. Accompanying this article is an illustration of Patanjali's chakras as lotuses (padmes), with the ultimate illumination around the top of the head. I'll explain his "threefold inner discipline" following these quotes:

> By the practice of the threefold inner discipline at the psychic center at the navel (the Manipura chakra) the knowledge of the physiology of the body is gained.
> By the practice of the threefold discipline on the light that appears in the crown of the head during meditation, one has the vision of sages who have attained perfection.
> By the practice of the threefold discipline on the spiritual heart [or the psychic heart center Anahata] there arises knowledge concerning the mind-stuff or the undivided intelligence.
> When there is loosening of the bondage of the consciousness to the body, as also an understanding of the proper channel of the consciousness's entry into and its withdrawal from the body, the mind acquires the ability to enter another body.
> When the vital force which maintains equilibrium and which fills the entire body with light, life and power, is directly perceived and understood, there is effulgence and radiance of one's personality.
> Beyond all these is the state of consciousness which is not the product of thought: and that is the cosmic intelligence which is independent of the body [or bodies: physical, astral, and causal]. By the practice of the threefold discipline upon that, the veil that covers that light of cosmic intelligence is removed. By the practice of the threefold discipline on the gross [tangible, with form] and the subtle [intangible, formless], and their conjunction, and the direct perception of their apparently substantial nature, there arises the perfect understanding of the elements that constitute that ex-

istence. What constitutes perfection of the body? Beauty, grace, strength, and diamond-like strength.

What is his threefold inner discipline? Patanjali explains it this way:

When the attention of the mind-stuff is directed in a single stream to a chosen field, without being dissipated and thus distracted that is **concentration**.

When the cognition is entirely concentrated in that field thus becoming its own field of observation—that is, when the observer is observed—it is **meditation**.

When the field of observation and the observing intelligence merge as if their own form is abolished and the total intelligence shines as the sole substance or reality, there is pure choiceless awareness without the divided identity of the observer and the observed—that is **illumination**.

When these three happen together there is perfect inner discipline. This can happen during what is commonly known as the practice of meditation, *and* during any other form of physical or mental activity.

When such inner discipline is mastered, there arises the vision that is **wisdom**. This vision (or the eye of intuition, or the eye of wisdom, or the inner light) can be directed to many fields of observation. These three are *inner* spiritual practices.

We have two nervous systems, the central and the autonomic. The central is often referred to as the cerebrospinal system, because it includes the brain, the spinal cord, and the nerves that spread from the spinal cord to all parts of the body. It also includes the somatic nervous system, which controls organs under voluntary control (mainly muscles). On the other hand, the autonomic system controls involuntary functions in the body. The autonomic system is composed of the sympathetic and the parasympathetic subsystems. The parasympathetic system is concerned with conservation and restoration of energy, as it causes a reduction in heart rate and blood pressure, and facilitates digestion and absorption of nutrients and the excretion of waste products. The sympathetic system enables the body to be prepared for fear, flight, or fight. Sympathetic responses include an increase in heart rate, blood pressure, and cardiac output, a diversion of blood flow from the skin and splanchnic vessels to those supplying skeletal muscle for above-normal strength, increased pupil size for above-normal vision, bronchiolar dilation for above-normal breath, and metabolic changes, such as the mobilization of fat and glycogen for an immediate energy supply.

In Yoga, these two systems are the sushumna and the combo-team of ida and pingala (parasympathetic and sympathetic). These are the major pathways of the life force in the body when the body is being used for spiritual purposes.

We must add to these two nervous systems the endocrine glandular system. This system has seven main locations, but each has many important interrelationships. The endocrine glands secrete the powerful hormones directly into our bloodstream, causing all manner of changes in the body.

In Yoga, the endocrine glands correlate to the seven spiritual centers (chakras and lotuses) in the body temple. When these centers are enlivened by the flow of the life force upward, or inward, they secrete messages that help create a more spiritual condition in the human body, with increased, rejuvenating energy and higher vibrations.

Finally, we need one more physical tool inherent in the human body for creating a spiritual condition, and that is breath. Breath in the physical is life.

Using these physical systems, we can move ourselves from our normal physical condition to a spiritual condition. Once in the spiritual condition, our body and mind are affected, resulting in significant change, and illumination eventually comes as from out of nowhere. The bliss of meditation—the ecstasy of being spirit-filled, the peace of the Infinite Consciousness—is the fruit of this ancient practice.

8

The Tao

*T*he word "Tao" (pronounced "dow") literally means "The Way." Taoism began about 600 BC, but its formal origins are generally attributed to the philosopher Lao–tzu and his book *The Way of Power*. In this text he presents the concepts of inaction and spiritual harmony.

Taoism has gone through many changes over the past 2,600 years. It can be divided into two branches; one seeks a way to physical and social health and well–being, and the other seeks a way to eternal reality and immortality. They work together because a healthy physical self makes an excellent temple for an enlightened mind and immortal spirit.

Transcending Taoism was devoted to conforming to the Law of cause and effect (karma) while breaking free of the bonds of illusion and confusion. Much of this transcendence was realized through contemplative meditation, breathing exercises, and reversing the flow of energy in the body and the thoughts in the mind.

There are eight stages along *The Way*.

Eight Stages to Immortality and Contentment

In *The Book of Consciousness and Life*, written in 1794 by Liu Hua–yang and later published in the popular *Secret of the Golden Flower*, there are eight stages to immortality and ultimate contentment. Liu Hua–yang begins each stage with a poetic instruction. Each contains attitudinal instructions for the mind and physical activities for the body. The overarching teaching for all of these stages is that all *activity* should lead to *non-activity*, all *thinking* to *non-thinking*, because, in this still state, we will reconnect with our true self, the primordial heaven from which we have come, and rebalance the physical and mental energy for eternal life.

Stage 1—Cessation of Outflowing

If thou would complete the diamond body with no outflowing,
Diligently heat the roots of consciousness and life.
Kindle light in the blessed country ever close at hand,
And there hidden, let thy true self always dwell.

"Heat the roots of consciousness and life" is both a physical and mental practice. Physically, it refers to awakening our root chakra and reversing its energy flow. Mentally, it refers to contemplation upon the genesis of our existence and our original nature. Who am I? What is my true "I am"? And how does my little "I am" correlate to the great "I AM"? As Plato posted above the entrance to his school: "Know Thyself."

This Taoist poet and teacher is guiding us to "kindle light in the blessed country ever close at hand"; meaning our *inner* consciousness and *inner* body's spiritual centers (chakras, sushumna, ida and pingala). He instructs us that this is a hidden place where our "true self always dwells." Fundamental to this first stage is completing our "diamond body" by turning within to the original source of life. This diamond body is analogous to Jesus' teaching that we must be "born again." We've been born physically; now we must conceive, gestate, and give birth to our spiritual, eternal, true self.

Stage 2—Circulation in Conformity with the Law

If one discerns the beginning of the Enlightened One's path,
There will be the blessed place of the West.
After the circulation in conformity with the Law,
There is a turn upward towards Heaven when the breath is drawn in.
When the breath flows out, energy is directed towards the Earth.
One cycle consists of six intervals.
In two intervals one gathers Sacred Energy.

The great Way comes forth from the center.
Do not seek the primordial seed outside!
The "blessed place of the West" is a poetic way of saying what we Westerners would call the Latter Days, the place of the setting sun, the end of an era. In other words, if we discern our enlightened soul's path, we will see where it is ultimately headed: back to heaven, back to the Father, as Jesus taught at the Last Supper. We'll also see that the bodily path of the Enlightened one is along the kundalini channel, which Edgar Cayce encouraged us to awaken to and use.

"After the circulation in conformity with the Law" is both physical and mental. It is a physical technique for raising the energy of our body through the kundalini pathway. This practice does not seek to raise the kundalini energy, or life force, in our body but to circulate it. The teacher points out that when we inhale, "there is a turn toward heaven." When we exhale, "energy is directed toward Earth." He states that it only takes two intentional cycles of inhalation and exhalation to gather the Sacred Energy latent in our body. Try this. Sit still; sense your deeper, true self and its eternal destiny. Then, as you inhale, draw the energy upward from the root chakra to the top of your head. Hold your breath there for a moment. Then, as you exhale, feel the energy flowing throughout your body, bathing its raised energy, sacred energy. Pause with the lungs empty and your focus on the root chakra. Feel the stillness. Then repeat the breathing exercise again.

Finally, in this stage the instructor guides us not to seek the primordial seed outside of us. It is, as Jesus and so many others have taught, within us.

Stage 3—Two Paths of Function and Control
There appears the way of the in–breathing and out–breathing of the primordial pass.

Do not forget the white path below the circulation in conformity with the Law!

Always let the cave of eternal life be nourished by the spirit-fire.

Ah! Test the immortal place of the gleaming pearl.

In this metaphorical stanza, the teacher is continuing the breathing exercise while encouraging us not to forget the deeper "white path below the circulation in conformity with the Law (as you sow, you reap; as you think, so you become). The white path is consciousness. Edgar Cayce often pointed out to highly advanced souls that they needed to be careful not to forget the difference between the "channel" and the "Creative Forces." Anyone can move the energy because the body is arranged for this, but what impelling force is beneath this energy? The pure white light of the Creator or self's ego?

The "cave of eternal life" is the deeper consciousness, beyond the conscious mind and the outer self's influence. Ezekiel told us that he could not find God in the lightning, the earthquake, or the thunder, but when he backed up to the mouth of the cave, he heard a still, small voice; and there was God. This Taoist teacher is saying the same thing. Nourish the cave of deeper consciousness with the fire of the spirit, both physically and mentally. Then, just as Jesus encouraged us to test the spirits, the Taoist teacher tells us to test the immortal place. See that it is the pure place, white light, true Creator of all. He compares this to a "gleaming pearl." A pearl is a good image for this. It is circular, as is the Sun disk, whole, the beginning and the end. It is made by dealing with the irritant of life's challenges, as the oyster deals with an irritating grain of sand. It gleams because the light is upon it.

Stage 4—The Embryo of the Way

According to the Law, without exertion, one must diligently fill oneself with light.

Forgetting appearance, look within and help the true spiritual power.

Ten months the embryo is under spirit-fire.

After a year the washings and bathings become warm.

Here the teacher is giving us the gestation period for our rebirth of the true self. He encourages us to help the inner development by budgeting time for the breathing exercises ("washings and bathings" are the intentional inhalations and exhalations, circulating the energy through the body) and by filling ourselves with light. In Egyptian mysticism, Hermes guides us to experience the inner mystical illumination through meditation and the outer reading and studying of inspirational writings. Cayce and the Taoists would add the outer *application* in our daily life activities of our inner experiences during inactivity, during stillness.

Stage 5—The Birth of the Fruit

Beyond the body there is a body called the Enlightened image.

The thought which is powerful, the absence of thoughts, is Light.

The thousand-petalled lotus flower opens, transformed through breath-energy.

Because of the crystallization of the spirit, a hundred-fold splendor shines forth.

Stage 4 states that after one year the embryo is ready for birth. Stage 5 is that birth. The breathing exercises and the raising of consciousness have opened the lotus flower and crystallized the spirit. Within the physical body and conscious mind are a new body and a new mind.

Stage 6—Retaining the Transformed body

Every separate thought takes shape and becomes visible in color and form.

The total spiritual power unfolds its traces and transforms itself into emptiness.

Going out into being and going into non-being, one completes the miraculous Way.

All separate shapes appear as bodies, united with a true source.

In this stanza the teacher gives insights into how to maintain the new body, the new mind. Just as the Psalmists of Western biblical thought, he addresses the "going out" and the "coming in" as our daily cycle. This cycle is "the miraculous Way." Day and night; wakefulness and sleep; activity and non-activity; thought and non-thought; form and formlessness; being and non-being are the rhythms that lead to reunion with a true source. Too much outer life, and we lose the Light to guide us. Too much inner life, and we cannot live the enlightenment to make it a living part of us. Budget time for inner and outer life. Oneness will eventually encompass both.

Stage 7—Face turned to the Wall

The shapes formed by the spirit-fire are only empty colors and forms.

The light of human nature shines back on the primordial, the true.

The imprint of the heart floats among the clouds; untarnished, the moonlight shines.

The boat of life has reached the shore; bright shines the sunlight.

Waxing transcendental, the teacher takes us into the upper reaches of infinite consciousness and life. His imagery is a poetic rendering of his personal experience with reunion to the true, the primordial, the shore of paradise.

In the final stage, he attempts to describe what cannot be described. It is the ineffable, transcending state of pure at–onement with the infinite, the universal, from out of which all life came and in which all life has its existence.

Stage 8—Empty Infinity

Without beginning, without end, without past, without future.

A halo of light surrounds the world of the Law.

We forget one another, quiet and pure, altogether powerful and empty.

The emptiness is illuminated by the light of the heart and of heaven.

The water of the sea is smooth and mirrors the moon in its surface.

The clouds disappear in blue space; the mountains shine clear.

Consciousness reverts to contemplation; the sun-disk rests alone.

Tibetan Mysticism

*I*n his book *Foundations of Tibetan Buddhism*, Lama Govinda, the English–man who became a full Tibetan Lama, writes that the word *mantra* is a combination of two elements. Its first element (*man*) comes from the root word in Greek (*menos*) and Latin (*mens*) that means "to think." Its second element (*tra*) comes from the suffix that forms tool words. There-fore, mantra is a "tool for thinking." But the word's original language was Sanskrit, and in this language it may be literally translated "mind protection," in the sense that a mantra helps the user protect the mind from ordinary thought and focuses the mind on higher ideals, higher perceptions.

A mantra can be a single word or word sound or a series of words or sounds. It is to be repeated during meditation. In some practices the mantra is chanted over and over, creating an altered state of conscious-ness in the singer.

The great Tibetan mantra is Om Mani Padme Hum.

Examining this mantra may give us further insight into the nature and the way to a deeper meditation and greater soul growth. Some translate these words as "Hail to the jewel in the lotus," but there's much more to this chant.

It is said that all the teachings of Buddha are contained in this man-tra. The leader of Tibetan Buddhists, the Dalai Lama, explains: "The six syllables of om mani padme hum mean that in dependence on the practice of a path which is an indivisible union of method and wisdom, you can transform your impure body, speech, and mind into the pure exalted body, speech, and mind of a Buddha [awakened one]. It is said that you should not seek for Buddhahood outside of yourself; the substances for the achievement of Buddhahood are within."

Let's examine this greatest of all Tibetan mantras.

Om

Om is actually three sounds in two letters. It has been written "Aum" at times in order to convey its three sounds. One might think of it as the Trinity: three in one. This sound is considered to be primordial, the first sound uttered by the Creator, a sound used to create the manifested cosmos.

Lama Govinda explains that "since Om is the expression of the highest faculty of consciousness, these three elements are explained accordingly as three planes of consciousness: 'A' as the waking consciousness (*jagrat*), 'U' as the dream–consciousness (*svapna*) and 'M' as the consciousness during deep sleep (*susupti*). Om as a whole represents the all-encompassing cosmic consciousness (*turiya*) on the fourth plane, beyond worlds and concepts—the consciousness of the fourth dimension. The expressions waking consciousness, dream–consciousness, and deep-sleep consciousness should however not be taken literally, but as: 1. The subjective consciousness of the external world, i.e., our ordinary consciousness; 2. The consciousness of our inner world, i.e., the world of our thoughts, feelings, desires, and aspirations, which we may also call our spiritual consciousness; and 3. The consciousness of undifferentiated unity, which is no more split into subject and object and rests completely upon itself. In Buddhism it is described as the state of unqualified emptiness (*sunyata*)."

With this in mind, the "Om" portion of the great mantra becomes a tool for making passage through levels of consciousness. "A-u-m" takes us from our outer self to our inner self, to beyond divided self into undifferentiated unity or oneness—that word that so many meditators use to describe their experiences in meditation.

Mani

Mani literally means "jewel." It may be compared to the philosopher's stone of the Western world. The philosopher's stone, first mentioned by Zosimos the Theban (ca. 250–300) in the third century, was considered to be a mystical substance that could turn base metals into gold, it could bind minds and souls into oneness, it contained the secrets of life and death, and could bring health to any who possessed it.

Interestingly, Mani also has three parts to it and is often called the "three-fold jewel" (tri-ratna). The three aspects are enlightenment, truth, and community.

The jewel is the mind. The first verse of the *Dhammapada* (a collection of 423 verses containing the Buddha's essential teachings) begins: "All things are preceded by the mind, led by the mind, created by the mind." In a story about an ancient guru, the yogi instructs a king who is seeking enlightenment to focus on his jeweled bracelet: "Behold the diamonds of your bracelet, fix your mind upon them, and meditate thus: They are sparkling in all the colors of the rainbow; yet, these colors, which gladden your heart, have no nature of their own. In the same way our imagination is inspired by multifarious forms of appearances, which have no nature of their own. The mind alone is the radiant jewel, from which all things borrow their temporal reality."

Mind, however, has two aspects, one individual and one universal. This meditation mantra/chant is intended to help the mind awaken to the universal consciousness. Once universal consciousness is known, then one must hold the balance between empirical-individual mind and the universal-spiritual mind. The greater balance is found when the universal consciousness experiences itself through individuality, seeing in the multiplicity of things and sensations the universal. A balanced oneness then becomes a center around which consciousness exists.

Despite the wonder of enlightened mindfulness, Lama Govinda believes that the jewel of the mind cannot be found anywhere except in the lotus (*padme*) of one's own heart.

Padme

Padme literally means "lotus." The lotus is a symbol of enlightenment. Out of some of the darkness of mud pools may grow some of the
most beautiful lotuses. Out of the darkness of our consciousness may
grow enlightenment: first by lifting our consciousness above the muck,
as the lotus reaches beyond the mud into the air, then unfolding our
understanding as the lotus unfolds, one petal at a time. Out of human
nature may grow godliness. Out of materiality may come spirituality.
Out of form may come essence.

Lotuses do not grow in Tibet, yet even here the lotus is the symbol
for enlightenment.

The Tibetan Lama Govinda writes, "If the urge towards a higher consciousness and knowledge were not dormant even in a state of deepest
ignorance, nay, even in a state of complete unconsciousness, Enlightened Ones could never arise from the darkness of *samsara* [the finite
world]." Deep within the mud of earthiness lies the seed, the motiva-
tional spirit to rise up toward the light. Deep within each of us, this
same spirit longs to pursue its destiny.

The seven spiritual centers of the body are represented by wheels
(chakras) and lotuses (padmes). As wheels, they are energy zones. As
lotuses, they are points of consciousness. The energy and consciousness
can be lowered or raised. Each soul has the free will to do as it pleases,
yet in the face of its destiny and karma. But if the soul begins to long for
its true purpose for existence, for consciousness, then it will naturally
begin to seek the higher energy, the higher consciousness.

Hum

Hum is a complement to Om. The beginning of the mantra, Om,
harmonizes with the end of the mantra, Hum. The whole of enlightenment is realized in the union of these two.

Om is the infinite, the primordial essence out of which we have come
and to which we will return. Hum is the Om of the infinite expressed
in the finite. Hum is the timeless–eternal expressed in the momentari-
ness of this temporal life. Hum is the formless manifest in form,

the essence expressed in substance.

In the *Isavasya Upanisad* it is written: "In darkness are they who worship only the world, but in greater darkness they who worship the infinite alone. He who accepts both saves himself from death by the knowledge of the former and attains immortality by the knowledge of the latter."

The *Isavasya Upanisad* teaches that life in the world and life in the Divine Spirit are not incompatible. This is the complementary nature of the Om and Hum portions of this mantra/chant.

Hum gives the enlightenment a channel into our outer lives and relationships. In this manner the infinite unites with the finite, the universal with the individual, the spiritual life with the physical life. True harmony and balance are realized, and a patience arises that passes all understanding. It is a patience that reaches beyond all problems, all temptations, all troubles. A contentment, a peace, grows in the place of balance between these two great realities—Om and Hum—each finding expression and consciousness. The two become one by virtue of their complementary existence.

Om Mani Padme Hum

10

Egypt's Seven Gates

*T*he following is a selected text from *The Book of the Master of the Hidden Places*, popularly called *The Egyptian Book of the Dead*. It is an initiation text. Try using it in a ceremonial manner as you prepare for a period of meditation. Use incense and candles, perhaps some bells or music. Special clothing may also add to the ceremonial nature of the initiation process. Each Gate is associated with a specific chakra or spiritual center. The words and thoughts are quite powerful. Wherever you see [Your Name], speak your name.

Gate 1: Root Center

Here begins the Entrance on Light and of coming forth from and going into the Territory of the Holy Dead in the beautiful Hidden Place.

Homage to thee, O Guardian of the Hidden Place. O you who make perfected souls to enter into the Temple of Reunion.

May you cause the perfected soul of the Reunited One, the seeker [Your Name], to be victorious with you in the Temple of Reunion. May he/she hear as you hear; may he/she see as you see.

O you who open the way and lay open the paths to perfected souls in the Temple of Reunion, open you the way and lay open the paths to the soul of Reunited [Your Name].

Homage to thee, O thou who art at the head of the Hidden Place.

Grant that I may arrive in peace in the Hidden Place and that the lords of the Ascent may receive me.

Gate 2: Navel Center

Here makes the Spirit Body to enter into the Upper Gate of the Ascent.

Homage to thee, O thou that dwellest in the Holy Mountain of the Hidden Place. Grant that I may arrive in peace in the Hidden Place and that the lords of the Ascent may receive me.

Here begins the Entering on Light and living after death.

Hail, One shining from the Moon! Hail, One shining from the Moon! Grant that the Reunited [Your Name] may come forth from among those multitudes which are outside; and let him/her be established as a dweller among the citizens of Heaven; and let the Hidden Places be opened unto him/her. And behold, Reunited One, Reunited [Your Name], shall Enter on Light.

Gate 3: Solar Plexus Center

Here begins the Passing over the Celestial Road of the Upper Gate of the Tomb.

The Resurrected Infinite One, triumphant, says: I open out a way over the Watery Abyss which forms a path between the two Combatants: Darkness and Light, Evil and Good, Death and Life, Law and Love, Selfish self and Reunited Self.

May a path be made for me whereby I may enter in peace into the beautiful Hidden Place. And may a path be made for me whereby I may enter in and adore the Reunited One, the Lord of Life.

Praise to The Attuned One when he rises upon the Horizon.

Gate 4: Heart Center

Here begin the praises and glorifyings of coming out from and of going into the glorious Inner World which is in the beautiful Hidden Place.

I am Yesterday, the Timeless One; I know Today.

What then is this? It is the Hidden Place wherein were created the souls of the gods when the Father was leader in the Mountain of the Hidden Place.

I know the God who dwells therein. Who then is this? It is the Reunited One.

What then is this? It is the horizon of his Father, the Unmanifested One.

What then is this? It is the cutting off of the corruptible in the body of the Reunited One, the earthly [Your Name]. It is the purification of Reunited [Your Name] on the day of his/her birth.

I pass over the way, I know the head [Crown Center] of the Pool [Navel Center] of the Well of Life.

What then is this? It is the gate, the door; and it is the northern door of the tomb [Crown Center].

Now as concerning the Pool [Navel Center] of the Well of Life, it is Abtu; it is the way by which his father, the Unseen One, travelleth when he goes forth to the Realms of Initiation.

Now the southern gate [second chakra] of the Ascent is the gate of the Pillars of He who rises. It is the gate where the god who rises lifts the disc of Heaven. The gate of the north [pineal center, beginning at the base of the brain and continuing through the brain to the third eye center] is the Gate of the Great God. The northern gate of the Ascent is the two leaves [the two hemispheres of the brain] of the door through which the Unmanifested god passeth when he goeth forth to the Eastern Horizon of Heaven [from the back of the head, over the crown of the head, and on toward the forehead].

Gate 5: Throat Center

Here begins the Entering on Light in the Inner World.

I am Yesterday, Today, and Tomorrow, the Dweller in Eternity, and I have the power to be born a second time. I am the divine hidden Soul who gives meals unto the citizens of the Inner World, the Beautiful Hidden Place and Heaven.

I am the Lord of seekers who are raised up; the Lord who comes forth from out of the unconscious.

Hail, Lord of the Shrine which stands in the middle of the Earth. He is I, and I am He. Make thou thy roads glad for me. Send forth thy light upon me, O Soul unknown, for I am one of those who are about to enter in.

Come thou who dwells above the divine Abyss of water.

The god who is the Conductor of Souls transports me to the Chamber of rebirth, and my nurse is the divine, double Lion–God himself, Yesterday and Tomorrow. I am made strong and I come forth like he that forceth a way through the gate. "I know the depths" is thy name.

I am he who Enters on Light. The doors of Heaven are opened for me; the doors of earth are opened for me. Hail, thou soul who rises in Heaven. Strengthen thou me according as thou hast strengthened thyself, and show thyself upon earth, O thou that returns and withdraws thyself.

Messiah, Redeemer, son of the Mother of all, avenger of the Father! Strengthen thou me, according as thou has strengthened thyself, and show thyself upon earth, O thou that returns and withdraws thyself.

Gate 6: Crown Center

Here begins the way of Causing the soul to be united to its body in the Inner World.

The Reunited [Your Name], triumphant, says:

Hail, thou god "the bringer"! Hail, thou god "the runner," who dwells in thy hall! Great God! Grant thou that my soul may come unto me from wheresoever it may be—NOW. [Pause here to receive the permission.]

Hail, ye gods . . . who make souls to enter into their spiritual bodies. Grant ye that the soul of Reunited [Your Name], triumphant, may come forth before the gods and that it may have peace in the Hidden Place. May it look upon its body and neither perish nor suffer corruption forever.

The paths which are above me lead to the gateway.

Open unto me!

Gate 7: Forehead/Third Eye Center

Here begins the Entering into the Hall of Double Truth.

And they say unto me, who art thou then? And they say unto me, what is thy name?

Come, then, they say, and enter in through the door of this Hall of Double Truth.

We will not let thee enter in through us, say the bolts of this door, unless thou tell us our names.

"Tongue of the Balance" of the place of right and truth is your name. [Pause to allow the doors to open.]

The heavens are opened, the earth is opened, the West is opened, the East is opened, the southern half of Heaven is opened, the northern half of Heaven is opened.

Now, here begins the Entering into Heaven.

The Attuned One lives, the Earth Bound One dies. Sound is he/she who is the chest, Reunion triumphant.

May those who build up grant that the Reunited [Your Name] shall arrive happily in the Hall of Double Truth. May He Who Makes Re-union to be Secret grant that the Reunited [Your Name] may be a lord of strides in the habitation of the Ascent. And there shall be made an offering by the Reunited [Your Name] when he/she enters through the hidden pylons.

May the company of the gods who rule over the Hidden Place grant that Reunited [Your Name] shall go in through the secret door of the House of Reunion. And there shall be made an offering by Reunited [Your Name] when he/she shall walk up the Great Staircase.

The Lady of the Hidden Place, mighty dweller in the funeral moun-tain, lady of the Holy Place, receive the Reunited [Your Name]. The At-tuned One liveth, the Earth Bound One dieth. Sound is he who is reunited triumphantly.—Amen.

We used this text in a ceremony at one of the annual Ancient Mys-teries Conferences at A.R.E. Headquarters in Virginia Beach, Virginia, with wonderful results. Almost everyone had an extraordinary experi-ence. It does help when done with others. But on your own it can also be profound.

11

The Judeo-Christian Temple

*F*rom his trance state, Cayce stated, "For the body is indeed the temple of the living God, and He has promised to meet you there, in the holy of holies, in the Mount within." (1152-2). And in 882-1, he said, "'There I shall meet you, in the Mount of yourself.' For your body indeed is the temple of the living God; there He may meet you as you turn within." In reading 707-6 we have, "Remember all that has been given as to the manner in which the individual finds self? Did Moses receive direction other than by the period in the Mount? Did Samuel receive other than by meditating within his own closet? Did David not find more in meditating within the valley and the cave? Did not the Master in the Mount and in the garden receive the answers of those directing forces?" "Why, you may ask, did the Master love to be in Galilee when the house of the Lord His God was in Jerusalem? Why did He love to be alone in the Mount?" (3357-2)

Going to the Mount of God, which is ultimately within us, is the manner by which we find God-consciousness. It is an *ascending* attunement, as going *up* on the Mount implies. It requires that we raise ourselves out of finite, individual consciousness into infinite, universal consciousness.

In reading 440-16 is a fascinating vision into that original experience on the Holy Mount: "They had seen the Lord Jehovah descend into the

Mount, they had seen the Mount so electrified by the presence of the od of the people and ohm of the Omnipotent to such an extent that no living thing could remain on the Mount, save those two [Moses and Joshua] who had been cleansed by their pouring out of themselves to God, in the cleansing of their bodies, in the cleansing of their minds." Cayce's reference to the "od of the people" refers to a term coined by Reichenbach (1788–1869) to explain an unseen force in nature that manifests itself in magnetism, hypnotism, and light called the "odic force." "Od," most likely derived from the Greek word *hodos*, meaning path or way, is used in such modern electrical words as *anode* and *cathode*, indicating poles of an electromagnetic field or ray (as seen in a cathode ray tube). Cayce's use of the word "Ohm" is probably referring to the term coined by one of Reichenbach's contemporaries, Georg Simon Ohm (1789–1854). This term is used today as a measurement of electrical resistance. However, the way Cayce used the term seems to equate *ohm* directly with *electricity*. Therefore, we could translate this Mount experience as "the magnetism of the people's hearts and minds seeking God so long and so hard as to attract the Omnipotent to descend upon the Mount. The nature of the Omnipotent is best equated to the powers of electricity, powers which may destroy or enlighten, depending on how pure the conductor (Moses)."

Cayce also correlates the Mount with the crown chakra of the body, located at the top of the head, the soft spot at birth. This idea is also found in a Hopi legend, which tells how the Hopi were guided by God to the new world, the guidance coming through the area of the soft spot on top of their heads. The crown chakra, the pineal center, is the sacred mount within us. Raise our energy and consciousness to this area, wait quietly upon the Spirit, and guidance will come to us.

St. Paul asked, in 1 Corinthians: "Don't you know that you are a temple of God, and that the Spirit of God dwells in you?" and "Don't you know that your body is a temple of the Holy Spirit which is in you, which you have from God?" In 2 Corinthians, he comes right out and says it plainly: "We are a temple of the living God; even as God said, 'I will dwell in them, and walk in them; and I will be their God, and they shall be my people.'"

The disciple John alludes to this when he recounts in his gospel an event when Jesus was in the great temple in Jerusalem and was asked to show the people a sign. "Jesus answered them, 'Destroy this temple, and in three days I will raise it up.' The people at the temple said, 'Forty–six years was this temple in building, and will you raise it up in three days?' But he spoke of the temple of his body."

From Edgar Cayce's attunement to the Universal Consciousness, he, too, saw and taught that our bodies are more than physical vehicles for living in this world. Here are five brief excerpts:

> Know that your body is the temple of the living God; there you may seek communion. There you may seek counsel as to the choices to be made, the directions to be taken.   622-6

> He has promised. 'If you will but open the door of your conscious-ness, of your heart, I will enter and abide with you.' This is not a fancy; this is not hearsay. You may experience such. For it is the law, it is the way, it is *Life* itself!   1632-5

> Seek and you shall find. Not without but from within. For in thine own temple He has promised to meet you.   2677-1

> All that you may learn of the Father God is already within self. For your body is indeed the temple of the living God, and as you meet Him there you may gain in your own consciousness the satisfaction of walking and talking with Him. When these consciousnesses are yours and you are one with Him, then indeed may you see that the kingdom of heaven dwells within.   5155-1

> This is a promise to you, to each soul; yet each soul must of itself find that answer within self. For indeed the body is the temple of the living God. There He has promised to meet you; there He does. And as your body, your mind, your soul is attuned to that divine that answers within, so may you indeed be quickened to know His purpose; and you may fill that purpose for which you entered this experience.   622-6

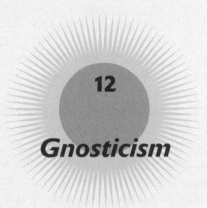

12

Gnosticism

Since the discovery of the Gnostic Gospels in Egypt, much has been made of the role of the Gnostics in the growth of spiritual understanding. Therefore, let's take a closer look at some of the key teachings in Gnosticism.

Meaning and Origin

Since *gnosis* means "knowledge" and *gnostikos* means "good at knowing," Gnostics were "people who knew." In Gnosticism, salvation came through *knowing* the truth, and this truth would set one free.

The origins of Gnosticism are difficult to pinpoint. Some believe that it began with Hermes and the Trismegistic literature of ancient Egypt, which reflects many Gnostic principles and stories. Others believe that it began with a blending of Persian and Babylonian religious thought, when the Persian ruler Cyrus entered Babylon in 539 BC. Many ancient tablets have been found to support this hypothesis. Still others point to the Greek aspects of Gnosticism and consider that it began with Alexander the Great and his general Ptolemy. Others say that Gnosticism is a mystical outgrowth of Judaism, because many of the tablets unearthed in Assyria and Babylonia use terms and names of unmistakable Semitic sounds and words. Since there were many cultured Jewish colonies in the Euphrates valley (Babylon), this early origin is an under-standable choice.

There is good evidence to support each of these hypotheses, so per-haps Gnosticism's roots lead back into all of these ancient cultures and locations. Whatever its origin, we know that it existed late into the fifth century AD and that for some uncertain reason, Gnosticism completely adopted Christianity when it came along. This was not a localized phe-nomenon but spread throughout all Gnostic communities, from Spain to Persia, from Greece to Egypt. One reason ancient Gnosticism was inclined to accept Christian thought was the belief in a savior. From very ancient times, Gnostics held that the "Good God" was going to send a powerful savior, a *Soter*, who would bring order out of chaos and open the way to salvation. Jewish Messianic beliefs fit right in with their own. However, several sects of the Gnostics could not accept Jehovah as equivalent to their Good God. For reasons not clear from the extant literature, Gnostics accepted unequivocally that Jesus was indeed their long-awaited Messiah, Savior, *Soter*. They adopted and practiced Chris-tian sacraments, including baptism, confirmation, communion, and a uniquely Gnostic sacrament called *Nymphon*, literally meaning "bride chamber," which was a ceremony whereby they wedded their souls to their angels, or the spiritual portion of themselves that remained in heaven—basing this on Jesus' parable about the bridegroom. So enthu-siastic were the Gnostics about Christianity that they actually flooded the then world with esoteric Christian literature, including apocryphal Gospels, Acts, and Apocalypses. For the first few hundred years of Chris-tianity, there was more Gnostic Christian literature than traditional Ro-man–Byzantine Christian literature. But the Christian Church today considers all Gnostic teachings to be non–Christian.

Principle Teachings

Because of the multiplicity, complexity, and divergence of Gnostic thought, it is impractical to detail all of its teachings. It would also be a confusing collection of terms, names, and tales. The following is a sum-mary of the most widely held and the most classical Gnostic concepts and stories.

Fundamentally, Gnosticism holds that matter, or physicality, is a de-terioration of spirit, and the whole of the universe a deprivation of the Divine Ideal. The ultimate end of all being is to overcome the grossness of matter and the physical world and return to the Mother–Father Spirit. Such a victory over matter and a return to the Creator will be inaugu-rated and facilitated by the appearance of the God–sent Savior. Gnostics believed that physical existence is essentially evil, resulting from a flaw or sin, and that it is the duty of every soul to overcome this material influence, escape it, and return to the Spirit–Parent.

Cosmology

According to Gnosticism, there was first the "Depth," which may be compared to the infinite, *unseen* universe. Then there was the Fullness of Being (*bythos pleroma*), which is comparable to *nonphysical* components of the cosmos, such as the *thought* of light, stars, galaxies, planets, moons, and so on—not the physical form of these but their essence, their spirit, the thought of them. Amid these was Non–Being God (*ouk on theos*), a "Universal Consciousness." Then there was the Creator, who is called First Father (*propator*). Initial consciousness sprang from First Father's depths. First Father conceived the central Monad (*monas*), an indivisible *oneness* that pervades all life, seen and unseen. This Monad is compa-rable to the "Logos, "the "Word"—as the disciple John wrote: "In the beginning was the Word, and the Word was with God, and the Word was God. All things were made through this One." There is a First Source (*proarche*), which may be compared to Cayce's "First Cause." There is also Unknown God (*hagnostos theos*), sometimes called Unknown Father and, at other times, the Good God. Humankind (*anthropos*) came out of the indivisible oneness of the Monad.

Light Emanations

From Good God (Unknown Father) emanates a number of pure spirit forces. They are called by different names, depending upon which group is teaching (for example: aions, syzygies, sonships, light–kings, etc.). For our purposes here, we'll refer to them as Light Emanations. Even though there are many different names for them, the concept of *emanation* is common to all Gnostic sects. The number of Light Emanations varies widely, some numbering them in the thirties. Light Emanation is similar to the Egyptian concept of the one god RA (pronounced *Ray*) emanating *rays* of light that have specific functions throughout the creation. One major Gnostic group teaches that the Light Emanations came in pairs: first, Depth and Silence, which produced Mind and Truth; these then produced Reason and Consciousness, and ultimately Man and Condition (or Circumstance, possibly akin to the Hindu idea of *dharma*).

The Light Emanations are not physical. They are purely ideals, hypostatic thought forms of the supersensible dimensions. Together with the source from which they emanate, they form what is called "the Fullness of Being."

The story goes that the transition from non–material life to material, physical life was the result of a flaw or a passion or even a sin in one of these Light Emanations. Of course, the Light Emanation most likely to have such a flaw was the pair Man and Condition. Many Gnostic groups teach that the flaw was indeed in the last Light Emanation. Some groups have a story akin to the Lucifer legend in which the most beautiful Light among the emanations fell from grace, just as Lucifer, the most beautiful angel in heaven, fell from grace.

The ultimate end of all Gnosis (knowledge) is *mentanoia*, which means something like "making amends" to undo the flaw that led to material existence and returns one to the Fullness of Being.

Wisdom and Chaos

There are many different Gnostic stories about the cosmology and creation process. Some of the richest are developed around the tales of *Sophia* (sometimes called *Achamoth*). She is the Light Emanation of Wisdom, specifically the "Wisdom from above" (*he ano Sophia*). But she is also a female spirit (*he kato Sophia*). In her ideal essence she is the "Lightsome Mother" (*he Meter he Photeine*). In her lower state she is the "Lustful One" (*he Prouneikos*), a once virginal goddess who fell from her original purity. A Gnostic magical chant used to protect one from corrupt emanations reveals the dual aspect of Sophia, calling upon her higher nature while subduing her lower nature: "I am a vessel more precious than the female who made you, if your mother ignores the source from whence she is. I know myself, and I know from whence I am and invoke the incorruptible Sophia, who is the Father, the Mother of your mother, who has neither father nor husband. A man–woman, born from a woman, has made you, not knowing her Mother, but thinking herself alone. But I invoke her Mother."

Sophia is the primal feminine principle in the universe and is the counterpart to the Unknown Father, who is the primal masculine principle in the universe.

One story tells how her great love for the Unknown Father drove her to seek to know him and to comprehend his greatness. However, such a realization would have ultimately meant the dissolution of her being into the immensity of his infinite nature. Fortunately, she was saved from falling into the abyss of infinity by a "Boundary Spirit." These spirits are stationed throughout the cosmos to guide, guard, and help.

After the creation began, Sophia perceived the inevitable chaos that would result as multiplicity overwhelmed oneness and endless layers of subsequent creations spun on and out from the original. To bring order to the chaos, she created the material universe and specifically our Solar System (*Hebdomad*), which is known as "the Seven Heavens." Therefore, she is "the mother of the seven heavens." Keep in mind that she is not physical, and the seven heavens are not in matter yet but only in spirit.

It is said that her concern over the chaos of multiplicity caused her to hurry back into the depths of the Unknown Father (but not losing herself in his immensity), and the union with him produced an offspring (while maintaining her virginal goddess condition, of course). This story has similarities to that of the Egyptian goddess Isis, who sought to conceive a messiah for earth, also without conjugal intercourse. However, unlike Isis, who produced the messiah godling, Horus, Sophia projected a "formless substance," which some believe may have been *ether*, the fifth element—not one of the four physical elements: earth, water, fire, and air. As you may know, Cayce's readings correlate ether with the Akashic Records, which are on "the skein of time and space." In this way Sophia may be considered the creator of the essence that would ultimately result in the material universe and matter, including time and space.

In a story found in the *Pistis Sophia* (chapter XXIX), Sophia originally dwelt in the highest heaven (the thirteenth) but was seduced by a demon who used a ray of light that she mistook as an emanation from the First Father. She pursued this light. It led into Chaos below the twelve Lights (or heavens), where she was captured and imprisoned by the dark powers. This is similar to the Mayan tale of how the Lords of the Underworld tricked the Gods of Light, capturing and imprisoning them in the underworld and keeping them distracted with games and challenges that they rarely won.

Christ, Holy Spirit, and Savior

After Sophia has fallen from the highest heaven and become captive in matter, the Unknown Father, the Good God, emanates two new Lights, Christ and the Holy Spirit! Christ and the Holy Spirit take hold of Sophia's "formless substance" and give it essence and form, whereupon Sophia tries to rise again to the Father, but in vain. To help her, the Unknown Father emanates the Savior, who must come down into the realms of matter and unite himself with the man Jesus, the son of Mary. Man is seen as a compound of body, soul, and spirit. His salvation consists in the return of his spirit (*pneuma*) to the Fullness of Being. However, if he is only a *psychicist*, not a full Gnostic, his soul (*psyche*) returns only to his Mother, not to the fullness found in the combination of the Mother and the Unknown Father.

The Savior's light illuminates predisposed souls moving down the stream of time and space, igniting the truth that lies dormant within the inner recesses of their being. The Gnostic Savior is not a man but a Light that entered a man, Jesus, and manifested through him for all to see. The Gnostic Savior is the Holy Spirit that was *in* Jesus, rather than the man Jesus. A distinction that Cayce also makes: Jesus is the man; Christ is the spirit.

The Good God is seen as the opposite of the World–Creator, or the Lord of this World, who captures and imprisons souls. The Good God revealed himself to Jesus; to know Jesus and his gnosis (knowledge) is to become entirely free of the yoke of the World-Creator.

The Cosmic Process

Gnostic salvation is not just an individual redemption of each soul but *a cosmic process* through which each soul must learn the whole truth. The process is quite structured and is associated with the planets in this solar system—as the Cayce readings also indicate.

Sophia is the mother of the seven heavens and wisdom; therefore, when a soul finishes its journey through the seven heavens, the implication is that it has achieved sufficient gnosis to redeem itself from the captivating power of form over essence. The seven heavens, as given to us by the Gnostic writer Origen (Contra Celsum, VI, xxxi), are in this order: the heavenly realm of Saturn (*Jaldabaoth*, which may be interpreted as "Child of Chaos"); Jupiter (*Jao*, which may be derived from the Gnostic magical word *iao*—more on magical words later); Mars (*Sabaoth*, which is an Old Testament title meaning "God of Hosts"); Venus (*Astrophaios*, associated with the feminine principle); Sun (*Adonaios*, meaning "Lord"); Mercury (*Ailoaios* or *Ailoein*, or in Hebrew *Elohim*, meaning "God"—which indicates how highly the mind was held in Gnosticism); and Moon (*Oraios*, which may simply mean "Light").

Gnostic salvation is the return of all things to what they were before the flaw in the sphere of the Light Emanations brought matter into existence and imprisoned a part of the Divine Light in the realm of darkness. The salvation process is universal and driven by forces of destiny. No one can avoid it. One can resist it and thereby achieve a lower level of illumination or even darkness, a darkness resulting from not knowing the truth.

Primeval Human

"Primeval Human" (*Protanthropos*) occupies a prominent place in several Gnostic systems. It is an emanation from one of the Light Emanations. It is the fundamental being before its differentiation into individuals. Its helpmate is "Perfect Knowledge." It is pure mind *before* it was darkened by contact with matter. One text explains: "There is a blessed, incorruptible, endless light in the power of the Fullness of Being that is the Father of all things, who invoked the First Human. This First Human, along with his Perfect Knowledge, emits "the son of Man" (*Euterantropos*). The Son of Man is the same being as First Human but *after* its differentiation into individuals. Following the creation of the Son of Man, everything sinks into matter, into physical form. Subsequent to the creation of the Son of Man, Adam (*Anthropos*) is created as the fourth (some say third) individualized physical prototype. This concept may be compared to Cayce's four root races, each being an improved physical body over the previous. The adamic bodies are quickly multiplied, to be occupied by descending souls coming out of the Spirit realms into matter.

In *Pistis Sophia* the Light Emanation "Jeu" is called the First Human. He is the overseer of Light, messenger of the First Precept (Rule). In the Books of Jeu this "great Man" is the King of the Light–Treasure, enthroned above all things—the goal of all souls. He is the ideal. In several systems, including the "Evangelium Mariae," Barbelo (sometimes *Barbeloth*, *Barthenos*, even *Parthenos*) is the Godhead in its female aspect. Barbelo has most of the functions of the highest Sophia (*he ano Sophia*, "Wisdom from above"). It is believed that in individualized, incarnate form, she was the wife of Seth, through whom the good lineage led to the eventual birth of the Savior.

Some Gnostics considered Seth to be the father of all spiritual men (*pneumatikoi*, meaning "good with spirit"), Abel to be the father of all psychic men (*psychikoi*, meaning "good with soul"), and Cain the father of all carnal men (*hylikoi*, meaning something akin to "good with flesh").

Rites and Sacraments

Baptism—All Gnostic sects had the rite of baptism, *daily* baptism. The ceremony included a seal or sign and an utterance, sometimes a tablet with a mystic word on it. Here are two of the phrases spoken at the moment of the baptism: "In the name of the Unknown Father of all, in the Truth, the Mother of all, in him who came down on Jesus"; or "In the name that was hidden from every divinity and lordship and truth, which Jesus the Nazarene has put on in the regions of light."

Confirmation—The anointing of a candidate with odoriferous ointment or oil is the Gnostic sacrament of initiation. There is some indication that the Gnostics did not so much intend to evoke the Holy Spirit
upon the candidate as to seal him or her against the attacks of the dark
forces or drive them away by "the sweet odor which is above all things"
(*tes uter ta hola euodias*). The chrism (christening oil or ointment) usually
came from Balsam, because it was believed that it flowed from the Tree
of Life, and was mystically connected with the Cross. Anointing would
be accompanied with these words: "The hidden mystery in which the
Cross is shown to us."

Gnostics used oil sacramentally for many things, such as healing the
sick and anointing the dead. It was believed that the sacred odor of the
oil rendered the dead safe and invisible to evil powers during their
journey to the higher heavens.

Communion—Gnostics celebrated the "breaking of the bread." The use
of salt in this rite was important to them. It is believed that the disciple
Peter broke the bread of the Communion, and "putting salt thereon, he
gave first to the mother and then to us." The bread was always signed
with the Cross. Gnostics called the bread "oblation" (*prosphora*). Curiously, Gnostics often substituted water for wine. They even had a story
that at a communion led by Jesus himself, he set a fire, burned incense,
set out two flasks and two cups, one with wine, the other with water,
and asked the disciples to change the wine into water for the baptism.
This is a strange twist on Jesus' changing the water into wine at the
wedding and may be due to the Gnostic's belief in the fundamental evil
of flesh and blood, water being preferred, as it was a symbol of life and
cleansing.

Magic

All Gnostics believed in and practiced magic. They had numerous
magic spells, amulets, chants, charms, and diagrams. They believed that
the seven vowels were powerful magic. Uttering them or having them
written on a tablet or amulet called forth their power and protection.
Each vowel represented one of the seven heavens, and the whole of
them reflected the Universe. Without consonants, they represented the

Ideal and the Infinite not yet imprisoned and limited by matter. They also represented a musical scale, and many a Gnostic sheet of vowels was in fact a sheet of music, each vowel representing a note.

Diagrams were also magical. Circles within circles, squares, parallel lines, and so on, were considered to represent aspects of the cosmos. These were often combined with mathematical figures and names written within them. The universe was symbolized by a triangle enclosed in a circle.

The number 3 was the key to all mysteries. The three supreme principles are these: not-created, self-created, and created. The Savior has a threefold nature, threefold body, threefold power, and so on. Of course, the triangle has three sides and, in the diagram of the universe, represents the triune condition within the infinite circle. In this way multiplicity has been contained in a trinity, making it easier to know and regain the lost oneness.

Closing

Keep in mind that there were numerous Gnostic groups, each with its own variations of these concepts, stories, names, and terms. Gnostic writings were voluminous and complex, even confusing. What has been presented here is a distillation of its most relevant and helpful ideas.

13

Native American Visions

*L*ong before Spanish missionaries came to America, the Algonquin Indians believed in a vast, single "Great Spirit," *Kitshi Manitou. Manitou* can be translated to mean "supernatural" or "spirit," so we could translate this name as the "Great Supernatural," but "Great Spirit" is the common translation.

In the *Walam Olum* creation myth (attributed to the Delaware Indians), the supreme being of all *good* things is *Gicelamu'kaong*, who "created us through his thought" and entrusted his creation to such deities as the Sun, Moon, Thunder Gods, Four Winds, Earth Mother, and various masters of the animals.

The Pomo Indians of northern California call the most high god *Dasan*, identifying him as an ancestral father. They say that he "came out on the ocean and turned into a man. He talked, and by the power of his words, the world came into being. After this he made the first people." This is quite similar to the Christian idea that God became the "Word," and through the Word all things were created, and the Word became flesh (or man) and dwelt among us (see John's gospel, chapter one).

The Yahgan, or Yamana, Indians of Tierra del Fuego, a culture that has been estimated to be 8,000 years old, call the Supreme Being "Watauniewa," meaning "the old, eternal, unchanged One." As with many legends of the original, most high God, the Yahgan Indians consider the

Supreme Being not to be a creator but "the Creator of the Creator." This is similar to the Hindu idea of Brahman and Atman being two aspects of the Supreme God; the first aspect is apart from the creation, but the second aspect is actively involved in the creation. It also follows the previously mentioned Christian concept that the Word was with God and was God, but all things were created through the Word—implying that at least some aspect of God is not the creator.

The Haida Indians of the Northwest Coast actually call the Great Spirit "the power of the shining heavens." Across North America, natives of most tribes consider the sky, especially the *night* sky, the abode of the Great Spirit. The Oglala Dakota Indians consider all the heavenly objects to be distinct in their functions but united in the "Wakan Tanka," which may be translated as the "great holy." Let's briefly explore these heavenly places.

The Heavens and the Milky Way

Many Native Americans believe that the Milky Way is the heavenly place out of which all souls have come and to which all souls return. To some, the Milky Way is the "Happy Hunting Ground"; to others, it is the "River of Souls." To Bolivian Indians, the Milky Way is considered to be "the path of souls to the land of the dead."

Some mission Indians in California regard the Milky Way as a mystical world soul, akin to the Great Spirit, the Supreme Being, of which the breath, or soul, of each human is a star in the Milky Way. Egyptians have the same concepts, even painting stars on their ceilings to represent that stellar part of everyone who walks the halls of their ancient tombs and temples.

According to the Kwakiutl Indians on Vancouver Island, the Milky Way is the cosmic pole, connecting it with the many pole rituals found among North American Indian tribes. The cosmic pole is a connecting link between heaven and earth, frequently utilized by medicine men. And since the Milky Way is the abode of the dead, it is the way to one's ancestors and their help and guidance, making it one of the most powerful influences in the heavens.

Since the Milky Way splits into two clusters of stars, North American legends hold that there are different paths to the other worlds, and dissimilar fates after death. Legend holds that one road leads to heaven, the other to the underworld. Life beyond this world is dynamic and active, not passive and restive. Many Plains Indian tribes picture the dead as existing on a rolling prairie, which the Milky Way reflects in its sprawling splendor. Among the Indians east of the Mississippi, life after death is connected with maize (corn) cultivation and festivals, and the Milky Way is a reflection of the vast heaven field of maize as viewed from above (in other words, the stars are the tops of corn plants viewed from earth).

Venus

Mayans and Aztecs have many legends about their most important god, Kukulcan (Mayan) and Quetzelcoatl (Aztec), the winged–serpent god who becomes the morning star, Venus. They observed that Venus spends half of the year as the morning star preceding the sunrise, and the other half of the year as the evening star, setting after the Sun has been down for hours. This represents their god's power to bring more light into humanity's life. Fascinatingly, Pawnee priests believe that Venus brings life, strength, and fertility. And, as if some of the Pawnee were ancient Eastern mystics (coming from Mu), the Pawnee priests believe that Venus is the *yang*, or masculine, spirit in the morning, and the *yin*, or feminine, spirit at night.

Moon

In South America the moon is rarely associated with godly forces, but in North America it plays a significant part in lore, legends, and rituals. The moon is a divine force among the Eskimo, many of the Pueblo tribes in New Mexico, the Navajo, and Apache; the Zuni have the Moon Mother, and the Fox Indians regard her as a more amiable god than the Sun. The icon of the great feminine creator–goddess of the Shawnee is the moon. In most cases, the moon is a feminine spirit.

Sun

In almost all ancient cultures around the world, the Sun—the source of life, light, warmth, and the growing season—is representative of the Supreme God. It is so among most of the North American Indians too. Among the Gulf and Mississippi tribes, notably the Natchez, the Sun is the Supreme Being and, like the Egyptians' beliefs about Pharaoh, the Natchez priest–chieftains are considered to be divine incarnations of the Supreme God. The eternal flame, symbol of the Sun, burns in the chieftain's temple (reminiscent of the sacred fires of the Maya and Incas). Among most North American Indians, the Sun is masculine and the moon feminine except among the Algonquin, Cherokee, Yuchi, Seminole, and Eskimo cultures, who consider the Sun feminine.

High Places

Mountaintops, hilltops, mesas, or simply an area of raised land in an open plain were favored locations upon which ancient people constructed their sacred sites. The Incas of the Andean ranges believed that the higher the site, the more intense was its quality of sacredness (*huaca*). The Choctaw traditional name for ancient mounds is *Nanne-yah*, the "hills or mounts of God." Usually, the ancient people built an additional structure on these high places, from simple piles of rocks (reminiscent of the Tibetan *obo* heaps and Inca *apoceta* piles) to elaborate terraced altars and temples (such as the temple of Natchez, on a truncated mound, with elaborate steps of gradual ascent).

These high sites were used for festivals, ceremonies, and initiations. Individual and clan offerings, libations, sacrifices, and tithes were brought to these sites and offered to the forces of Nature or to their gods or to the supreme God or, in many cases, to the people's ancestors. Usually, these offerings were intended to give praise and honor as a form of worship and devotion. In some cases, the offerings were preparatory to receiving guidance or intercession for the clan or an individual. Among many cultures, these elevated places were also the burial grounds of their people, creating a natural inclination toward ancestor communication and worship. Sometimes, sepulchers were maintained in the rock surrounding the sites or in the earth or even in or under the altar or temple. Upon these high places, the clan's councils would hold their special gatherings and meet to ratify solemn covenants.

Some scholars have put forward the notion that so much smoke was generated by ceremonies and sacrifices that high places were much better choices than those low to the ground and near the people's camps, villages, or cities. Many ancient people considered rising smoke to be a means for carrying their offerings to the unseen heavens above. Many cultures used large quantities of incense in their altar fires, believing that the scent raised the people's consciousness and touched the gods' or ancestors' senses.

Throughout the Bible, we find sacred high places. In Hebrew the term for sacred high place is *bamah* (plural is *bamot*). In Assyrian it is *bamati*. The bamah was the holy place where the altar was located. Early on, it was a naturally high place; later, it could be an artificially elevated place. But it was always a place devoted to and equipped for the sacred activities of the people. The Arameans actually believed that the God of Israel was a mountain god, because the Israelites held so many ceremonies in the highlands. The list of sacred mounts throughout the history of the Israelites and other biblical groups is long, beginning with the most famous, Mt. Sinai, "the mount of God" (Exodus 18:5). To this mount, we can add Mt. Hor, Mt. Ebal, Mt. Carmel, Mt. Tabor, Mt. Olives (2 Samuel), and Mt. Ramah, where Saul and Samuel met. In 1 Samuel we find the Israelites holding council on the holy mount. In Exodus we find the people ratifying a solemn covenant on the mount. Aaron, the first high priest, was buried on Mt. Hor; Miriam on Kadesh–barnea; Joseph on Shechem; Moses on Nebo; supporting the idea that these high places were also burial locations. The Canaanites also believed that high places were the best locations for the people's sacred sites. Moabites worshipped Baal on Mt. Peor. Assyrians held their sacred ceremonies on the mountains in the northern parts of these ancient lands.

In the New Testament we again find high places used for sacred events: The Sermon on the Mount, the prophecy on the Mt. of Olives, and the Transfiguration on "a high mountain" (Matthew 17:1). In the Revelation, John tells us that an angel "carried me away in the Spirit to

a mountain great and high," and there he saw the city of God (Revelation 21:10).

On naturally formed mesas to manmade mounds, the people of
North America conducted ceremonies not only *on* these sites, but also
within them. As the Egyptian and Central American pyramids have inner chambers, so do many of the North American mounds. For example, in the King Mounds at Wickliffe, Kentucky, three rectangular
altars were found in chambers inside the mounds. (The concept of a
divine trinity is common among many of the world's religions and
among some Native Americans as well.)

The Inner Dimension

Why do we find high places with inner sanctuaries to be the favored
sites for sacred activities among the ancient people around the world?

The answer may be that a mount, mound, or elevated place reflects a
common human sense that God, heaven, and the forces for good are
above us; and conversely, evil, the underworld, and the forces of darkness are below us. We live in between.

But there is more to this. Going up to a high place reflected an *inner*
human belief that by separating oneself from the everyday, physical life
and its challenges, one could experience the higher, non-physical forces
of life—God or spirits or discarnate ancestors—for the purpose of receiving a message, some guidance, or an intercession against disease,
famine, or enemies that were affecting the incarnate peoples. In some
cases, going up to a high place was done for initiation of youth into the
deeper truths and unseen forces of the tribe, awakening within them a
connection with discarnate forces and resources.

Not only was the mound sacred, but the journey to the mound was
often an important part of the ritual, symbolically foreshadowing the
impending connection with the unseen forces. In ancient Egypt and in
Maya/Aztec and North American native rituals, the causeway, avenue
(as the Avenue of the Dead at Teotihuacan), or pathway leading to the
pyramid or mound was an important prerequisite to the ultimate experience on or within the sacred site. Before Moses went up on the mount
to meet God, he experienced many preparatory events that made it

possible for him to experience God directly. We can assume that a movement from normal consciousness to a heightened state of consciousness was required. That is, not only was God above him (upon the mount), but the way to God was within him in the form of a shift in consciousness—from individual, finite consciousness to universal, infinite consciousness.

Only the mind could take one in physical form to realms of the nonphysical, into the holy of holies, where God, the ancestors, and the unseen forces could speak as though face to face. Such a mental bridge is not the everyday mind but a deeper level of the mind that requires the seeker to shift from normal consciousness to one more capable of perceiving non-physical realms. This was often achieved by special rituals, drinks, or foods that would loosen the everyday mind's hold on consciousness or by creating a death-like experience that allowed the seeker to temporarily leave physical reality and reach into the other realms.

The Great Spirit and the sacred Mount are *within* us and may be accessed as in the days of old. Altered states of consciousness sought by ancient peoples may be ours through deep meditation and inner visions and dreams. Like the ancient peoples, we should set aside time for these sacred experiences. A little time each day or whatever you can allot for the practice will work wonders.

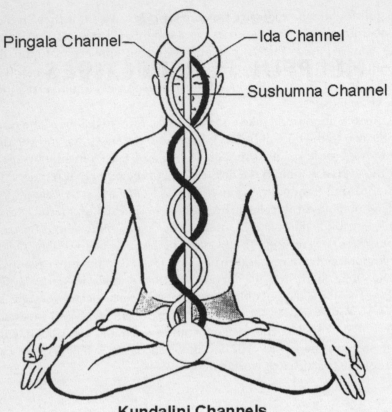

Pingala Channel —   — Ida Channel

— Sushumna Channel

Kundalini Channels

Section Three

HELPFUL PERSPECTIVES

14

Our Souls' Celestial Journeys

*I*t sounds so impossible, but we were once, and are forever, star travel-ers. We are only temporarily sojourning on this planet.

As much as we identify with planet earth and our terrestrial life, Edgar Cayce's reading of the Akashic Records and the Universal Con-sciousness tells a different story. From Cayce's perspective, we were, are, and will be again *celestial* beings, traversing the vast expanse of space. Our primal mission is to know ourselves and our Creator. Consider this reading, which I've edited for clarity, and focus on the point at hand:

As an entity passes on from this present time or this solar system, this sun, these forces, it passes through the various spheres—on and on through the *eons* of time or space—leading first into that central force known as Arcturus—nearer the Pleiades. Eventually, an entity passes into the inner forces, inner sense, then they may again—after a period of nearly ten thousand years—enter into the earth to make manifest those forces gained in its passage. In enter-ing, the entity takes on those forms that may be known in the di-mensions of that plane which it occupies, there being not only three dimensions as of the earth but there may be seven as in Mer-cury, or four in Venus, or five in Jupiter. There may be only one as in Mars. There may be many more as in those of Neptune, or they may

93

become even as nil—until purified in Saturn's fires. (Based on 311-2)

Cayce would begin soul readings for individuals by identifying their planetary and stellar influences, explaining that these were influences because of the souls' journeys through these dimensions prior to incarnating again. He explained: "As the entity moves from sphere to sphere, it seeks its way to the home, to the face of the Creator, the Father, the first cause." (136-8) Cayce identifies the first cause as this: "That the created would be the companion for the Creator." This is the reason we were created, and as a result, the created (our soul) is given opportunities to "show itself to be not only worthy of, but companionable to, the Creator." (5753-1) Since we are talking about the Creator of the entire cosmos and everything in it, we are celestial star travelers, even though we feel so earthly and terrestrial in our daily lives.

Cayce said that our taking many forms in many different dimensions and spheres helps us to experience the whole of our being and of our Creator's consciousness. He said that "self is lost in that of attaining for itself the nearer and nearer approach that builds in manifested form, whether in the Pleiades, Arcturus, Gemini, or in earth, in Arcturus, Vulcan, or in Neptune." (136-83) Yet, despite our taking on many "forms" as we manifest ourselves, our true nature is "as light, a ray that does not end, lives on and on, until it becomes one in essence with the source of light." (136-83)

Planetary Sojourns

Fascinatingly, Cayce gave specific activities that our souls experience in their journey in the realms of this very solar system we call home. In reading 311-2, he described them this way:

The common theory that incarnation into the earth plane is the only source of incarnation or appearance is erroneous, you see. When a soul enters in this present solar system's forces, the contacts or the relative relationships bear out the cycles of appearances in the various spheres of development; in Mercury, the *mental* life, its relative position to this solar system's center, making for those radiations in those forms which represent mental in its greater aspect. Then, in Venus the development is more in the form of *love*. In Mars and its radial effect or position about the solar center, make for those known as vengeance, wrath, madness, and such; and can one but know that each thought, each act, is that being builded. In earth we have that position in which matter takes all its various forms of pre-sentation of a given energy or force, as radiated from the various effects of this solar aspect, and take on *bodily* form, occupying a position of, as it were, three in one or all force in *this* sphere taking on that appearance of that known as threefold. In Jupiter taking on those ennobling forces, whether they be from earth, from Venus, from Mercury, from Mars, they are *broadened*, they are *changed* in their aspects, in their forms, as they are taken on in and about this sphere. In Saturn—that to whom all insufficient matter is cast for its remoulding. In the Uranian taking on those forces known in earth's plane as from occult influences—which makes for the accentua-tions of very good or very bad, and making for *extraordinary* condi-tions."   (Based on 311-2)

In reading 900–10 Cayce identified the planetary influences this way:

As in Mercury pertaining of mind; in Mars of madness; in earth as of flesh; in Venus as love; in Jupiter as strength; in Saturn as the begin-ning of earthly woes, that to which all insufficient matter is cast for the beginning. In that of Uranus as of the psychic; in that of Nep-tune as of mystic; in Septimus as of Consciousness; in Arcturus as of the developing.

In reading this passage, one is tempted to think that Septimus is Cayce's name for Pluto, but in reading 826–8, he said that Vulcan is Pluto. Septimus may well be the new object in our solar system that was recently discovered by California's Palomar Observatory and given the name "Sedna," after the Inuit goddess of the ocean.

Curiously, the Cayce readings reveal that we do not have to die physi-cally in order to travel to other dimensions. Sleep, which Cayce called the "shadow of death," affords our souls an opportunity to travel. Here's one example, in reading 3412-2 for a sixty-six-year-old homemaker: "As to the emotions from other sojourns, or the dream life of the entity, we find Venus, Mercury, Jupiter, Saturn and Uranus have brought those abilities." Some portions of our dream life are as real as our physical life and allow soul travel and other-dimensional experiences that influence our daily physical lives.

Arcturus and Other Solar Systems

Beyond the planetary soul journeys, Cayce gave many stellar journeys. The most important one was Arcturus. Arcturus claimed a special place in Cayce's cosmology: "Arcturus is that which may be called the center of this universe, through which individuals pass and at which period there comes the choice of the individual as to whether it is to return to complete in this planetary system—our sun, the earth's sun and its planetary system—or to pass on to others." (5749-14)

"For Arcturus is that junction between the spheres of activity as related to cosmic force. As those influences indicated in Atlantis were as a beginning, so Arcturus in the present might be termed as a beginning." (263-15)

Completing the Soul's Journey

When asked if it was "necessary to finish the solar system cycle before going to other systems," Cayce simply answered, "Necessary to finish the solar cycle."

When asked, "Can oneness be attained on any system, or must it be in a particular one?" He answered, "Depending upon what system the entity has entered, to be sure. It may be completed in any of the many systems." (Clearly, from Cayce's deep-trance attunement to the Universal Consciousness, there are "many systems" in which a soul can achieve oneness with its Creator and its purpose for existence.)

When asked, "Must the solar cycle be finished on earth, or can it be completed on another planet, or does each planet have a cycle of its own which must be finished?" Cayce answered, "If it is begun on the earth it must be finished on the earth. The solar system of which the earth is a part is only a portion of the whole. For, as indicated in the number of planets about the earth, they are of one and the same and they are relative one to another. It is the cycle of the whole system that is finished, see?" (5749-14)

Aliens Visiting Our Planet

In giving a past-life reading for a woman who had been a priestess among the Mayan people, Cayce casually mentioned that her Mayan incarnation was just prior to a period when earth was being visited by beings "from other worlds or planets." (1616-1)

> Hence the purposes in an experience are for the development of those forces and influences as to make or cause the whole of the entity's being—soul-body, soul-mind—to become more God-like, Christ-like, or Son-like. For we each are not aliens but sons and daughters of the Father, and we should manifest ourselves in such measures as to be worthy of same.   1483-1

15

We Are More Than We Imagine

*W*hen Edgar Cayce read the Akashic Records, he gave the most mar–velous descriptions of our abilities in Atlantis and other ancient cul–tures. For example, in his first reading of Mrs. 823's soul record, he said this:

> She was in Atlantis where she oft laid aside the physical body to become regenerated. She was among the priestesses of the Law of One, serving in the temples where there was the raising of the light in which the universal forces gave expression and brought for the body and mind the impelling influences. She was not only the priestess but also the physician, doctor for those peoples. The en-tity lived in Poseidia, in the temple, in the spirit influences of the material activities for some six thousand years—if counted as time now. (Based on 823-1)

She could rejuvenate herself so well that she lived for 6000 years! Cayce continues with this:

> With the last of the destructions that were brought about by the sons of Belial through the activities of Beelzebub, the entity jour-neyed with those people to the Yucatan land, establishing the

temple there. But with those inroads from the children of Om and the peoples from the Lemurian land, or Mu, the entity withdrew into itself; taking, as it were, its own flight into the lands of Jupiter.

Notice how casually Cayce speaks of the activities of Beelzebub! It's as if the Devil were an actual person, a being leading a band of bad guys, the sons of Belial. Apparently, they drove out our light–bearing priestess to Yucatan. Eventually, even Yucatan became a negative place, so she took flight to Jupiter! How cool is that! How often have you wanted to take flight out of here?

In reading the soul record for another amazing Atlantean, Ms. 3004, Cayce gave the following description:

The entity was in the Atlantean land, before there were the second of the upheavals, when there was the dividing of the islands [the continent of Atlantis broke into five islands]. The entity was among those that interpreted the messages that were received through the crystals and the fires that were to be the eternal fires of nature, and made for helpful forces in the experience of groups during that period.

When the destructions came, the entity chose rather to stay with the groups than to flee to other lands.

The unusual activities that may come with today's new developments in air and water travel, are not new to the entity; none of these are as surprises to the entity. For, these were the beginning of the developments at that period for the escape.

This lady then asked Cayce three very strange questions, but Cayce replied to each one with astonishing answers. These were her actual questions, as strange as they may be.

Q: What is the meaning of 532, the number on my forehead?
A: The number as indicated in self in the Atlantean experience, and that to which each of these numbers may attain.
Q: The Mene [a count of numbers, found in the Bible, such as "a time, times, and half time"] which is clearly written on my left eye?

A: This is as a part of the experience in the Yucatan activity as the priestess. Some call it the evil eye. Some call it the surety. What make ye of it? According to that for which ye may use same is the deeper meaning found in thine own self.

Q: And the double triangle between my eyes, just at the top of my nose?

A: This is a part of the experience to which the entity attained in the building, during the period of the Mound Builders.   3004-1

What a soul journey this lady had prior to her present incarnation. Here's the strangest part of this: in her present life she was a housewife in Pennsylvania—the great priestess of the Mound Builders, Yucatan, and Atlantis!

Consider one more reading.

When Cayce reviewed the records of 2464, a female art student at the time of the reading, he calmly gave this description:

In giving the interpretation of the records of the entity during the Atlantean sojourn, something of the history and something of conditions at the time should be comprehended—if the interpretation is to be in the consciousness of the present day experiences.

Through that particular period of experiences in Atlantis, the children of the Law of One—including this entity, Rhea, as the high priestess—were giving periods to the concentration of thought for the use of the universal forces, through the guidance or direction of the saints (as would be termed today).

Does this mean that the High Priestess was channeling the universal forces and the guidance from the saints in higher dimensions? It sure seems to be what Cayce is saying. He continued with her reading:

There are few terms in the present that would indicate the state of consciousness; save that, through the concentration of the group mind of the children of the Law of One. They entered into a fourth-dimensional consciousness—or were absent from the body. Thus they were able to have that experience of crystallizing, through the

Light, the speech from what might well be termed the saint realm,
to impart understanding and knowledge to the group thus gathered.   2464-2

No doubt now, the high priestess and her group were tuned to the higher, saintly realms and channeling guidance, understanding, and knowledge into this realm.

I could go on and on with Cayce readings like these, but now it is time to ask ourselves, What has happened to us? How have we fallen from such heights? How long will it be before we regain some of these abilities and awarenesses?

Actually, it's not as bad as it appears to be. Certainly, Cayce doesn't see our situation as poorly as we do. To Ms. 823, the 6000-year-old Atlantean priestess, he gave much hope and opportunity in this present incarnation and said that her activities in Atlantis and Yucatan were a part of her present-day abilities: "As a result of this incarnation [in Atlantis], she can create within herself the higher energies that are stored up from the emotional forces of the body to find regenerations in the lower form of electrical vibrations." Our priestess still had her regeneration powers within her.

One interesting point: Cayce connected her powers with "the emotional forces of the body." That is very interesting because in other readings, Cayce says that our past earth-life memories are in our emotions, while our past non-earth-life memories and influences are in our urges and dispositions. If we have an emotional reaction to someone or something, then it is likely a past-life connection. If we have an innate urge toward certain perspectives, activities, and interests, then it is likely that we have sojourned in dimensions associated with them. For example, our priestess flew to the "lands of Jupiter" after her Atlantean/Yucatan incarnation; therefore, she is likely to have innate urges toward large groups (the masses), expansiveness, high ideals, benevolent activities and perspectives, optimism, generosity, education, and so on—all astrological influences associated with the realms of Jupiter.

Let's return to Ms. 3004, who used the sacred fires and crystals to channel guidance into this physical world in Atlantis, Yucatan, and Ohio as the leader of some Mound Builders. To her, in this present incarnation, Cayce gave the following guidance and identified her present-day abilities.

> As the tenets of old, all the principles of the divine that are mani-
> fested in the material man are found deep within self. And all that
> we may know of a universal consciousness is already within self.
> But know thy ideal, that has been, that may be manifested in the
> material plane—spiritually, mentally, materially; and, most of all,
> know the Author of such ideas and ideals. Then, study to show
> thyself approved unto that chosen ideal; condemning none, but
> living, manifesting that ye profess to believe.
>
> In the organizations, in groups, in activities that have to do with
> historical facts, with legends, with ancient data, ye find the outlet
> for thy greater contribution to others. Thy greater help will be in
> aiding others to find themselves, not finding themselves through
> what any group or individual may believe but through what re-
> sponds to themselves.

Because of her diverse experiences and attunements in ancient times, she became a rare teacher and helper to those seeking to find them-selves.

A fascinating astrological influence in her present incarnation is iden-tified by Cayce as Uranus. Here's what he said about the effects of her sojourn in the nonphysical realms of Uranus between incarnations:

> Uranus makes for the interests in all matters pertaining to the occult,
> to the metaphysical, to the cosmos, to the universal consciousness,
> to that having to do with the basic cause or the reasoning of things.
> Thus not merely from the three-dimensional and that of lesson, or
> karma, but rather the cosmic consciousness becomes a part—as
> will be seen from the sojourns in the earth of this entity in those
> periods of activity in which there were undertakings that were to
> be a part of a universal consciousness of a peoples.   3004-1

Fascinating, isn't it? As I shared earlier, in this present life she was a housewife, but beneath her exterior lay the great high priestess of the

Atlantean crystal and fire altars, still able to reach into the realms of the saints and awaken within others their personal connection to the divine within. She even lifted them out of their karma into the higher perspectives of the universal consciousness.

Finally, let's look at what Cayce told Ms. 2464, the young art student who was once able to attune with her group of light bearers to the "realms of the saints." To her, Cayce gave this present-life ability: "As the entity in the future opens (as it has done in the past) those connections between the soul force and the spiritual force, the influences and activities in other than the three dimensions of materiality will become a part of the entity's experience. As we find, then, the entity is one very intuitive; easily separating self from itself—which so few may do; or, as it were, the ability to stand aside and watch self pass by. This is an experience that may be made to be most helpful, if there is first the determining within self as to what is thy ideal—spiritually, mentally, morally, socially or materially."

She was still powerful in her present life! She had within her all the powers she had had back in Atlantis, and they would open again. She might not have retained the title of High Priestess, but in this present life, she was still able to give the guidance and insight she had given in those glorious times.

As a weakness that she took from Atlantis, Cayce warned that she developed quite a temper toward the sons of Belial. He suggested that she be careful about reacting too negatively, even to evil. "In other words, with what spirit do ye declare thyself? That in conformity with the universal consciousness, the law of love? Or that of hate, dissension, contention—which brings or produces burdens upon thy fellow associates? For, the law of love is unchangeable; in that as ye do it to the least of thy fellows, ye do it to thy Maker." Sounds like the Master's guidance about loving even our enemies.

As to her present abilities with art (being an art student), Cayce gave the following: "Thus we find a highly emotional entity, one needing to keep itself literally—in body and mind—close to nature, close to the earth. Not as of the earth earthy, but as of the constant rebirth of those influences that so significantly indicate the closeness to God—and creative forces that are manifested in things, conditions arising from nature itself. For, the artistic temperament—with those abilities to draw on nature, as it were—brings the greater harmony, the greater balance within the experiences of the entity in its activity with things, conditions and people."

As for her present astrological influences (from sojourns in these nonphysical realms), Cayce gave these intriguing insights: "In Mercury and Venus we find those activities in which there is a high perception of ideals or tenets or ideas. Hence the artistic temperament towards the depicting of nature, or figures presented in nature; those things as would be of stone or plaster, or murals—as of decorations, should be a part of the entity's activities in the material associations with others. With Jupiter as well as Neptune, we find that these will bring the greater opportunities not only for self-expression but for giving ideas to others that may become helpful, hopeful influences in their experiences."

Obviously, from these three examples, you and I are probably better off than we realize. We have more power and wondrous capabilities than we realize. It's just that the physical world and life are often so mundane and fatiguing that we sink into the blues over our limited powers and often boring lives. We must shake this off, because latent within each of us is the ability to journey to the higher realms of consciousness and catch the energy and motivations that come with higher purposes!

How do we do this? First, we have to set aside some time in our lives for such activities and attunements. Now we might say that the ancient high priestess didn't have to wash clothes, clean dishes, make meals, mow lawns, drive the kids to activities, and so on; and we'd be right. Today we are all our own servants. In this respect, life in Atlantis was different. We might also say that we do not live for 6000 years any longer and 80 years goes by fast; and we'd be right. Life today is not like those ancient times in the temples and gardens. But the "sleeping" Cayce is clearly calling us to awaken to the power and awareness latent within us and to our important purposes for incarnating today, as indicated in his readings for these three Atlantean priestesses.

16

Our Electromagnetic Nature

A fascinating source for insights into the electrical nature of life is the American mystic Edgar Cayce. He demonstrated an unusual ability to get into a deep, trance-like state of consciousness in which he claimed to be in contact with a universal or collective consciousness. From this state he was able to perceive the physical condition of people, even people at great distances from him, and give them a course of action that would improve their health and, in some cases, heal them. On several occasions he also gave discourses on various topics and answered questions asked of him while in this altered state of consciousness. A fascinating aspect of his deep state was that he had to lie with his head and feet aligned with the magnetic fields of the earth! If he was going to give guidance on a health condition, he would lie with his head to the north and feet to the south. However, if he was going to give a discourse on a person's spiritual and mental condition, he would reverse these directions—head south, feet north. On a few occasions he was asked if he could retrieve information from the universal consciousness on ancient times and places. In these instances, he would lie with his head to the east and his feet to the west, apparently because time was somehow connected with the rotation of the planet. In order to go back in time, he needed to align himself with the time mechanism!

Here are some of his intriguing perspectives on the electrical nature of life, particularly human life.

Life Is Electrical

The study of electrical energies is the basis for finding in a scientific manner the motivative force of animation in matter. But in the study of this activity of electronic energy in man, look for it in the *lower* frequency and not in the ultra. For Life is, and its manifestations in matter are of an *electronic* energy.   440-20

Materiality or matter demonstrates and manifests the units of positive and negative energy, or electricity, or God.   412-9

Life itself is the Creative Force or God, yet its manifestations in man are electrical, or vibratory. Whatever electricity is to man, that's what the power of God is. Man may in the material world use God-force, God-power or electricity, to do man's work or to destroy himself.
                                                        3618-1

Know then that the force in nature that is called electrical or electricity is that same force you worship as Creative or God in action!
                                                        1299-1

The Electrical Body

Electricity is life in the nerve force of the body. Impressions produced through the sensory system act on the nervous system of the body. Relays of these are along the stations of ganglia or nerve centers along the spine and in the deeper nervous system. The relays of nerves to the sensory system are through the sympathetics (autonomic system). Those of the cerebrospinal system, or the spinal cord, are in the brain itself, or the ends through the oblongata.
                                                        131-1

Electrical forces from direct current will produce exaggeration or inflammation to the nerve walls. The reverse, or a cold electrical force, that is of low origin, produces a sullen, or acts as a sedative to the nerve force of the body. When we use electrical force in the nervous system, it should be of low origin or of cold storage or batteries applied along to the centers of the lymphatic circulation, to the armpits, ankles, or knee, and under them. Or the reverse current from static electricity along the spine or cerebrospinal forces. A positive suggestion to the mind as it goes to sleep will reach the sensory system by touch and hearing.   3990-1

Seeing this, feeling this, knowing this, you will find that not only does the body become revivified, but by the creating in every atom of its being the knowledge of the activity of this Creative Force or Principle as related to spirit, mind, body—all three are renewed. For these are as the trinity in the body, these are as the trinity in the principles of the very life force itself—as the Father, the Son, the Spirit—the Body, the Mind, the Spirit—these are one. One Spirit, One God, One Activity.   1299-1

Electricity is life; life is electricity, you see. Force or the power here in the atom in itself, which is the body drawn up, we have the electric force on the body will, if given into the nervous system, produce a reaction on the nerves themselves.   131-1

The Electrical Poles of the Body

The liver and the kidneys are the positive and negative poles of a human body, and when one of these becomes overtaxed, the other becomes supercharged in its functioning.   137-81

Now, as to the activities of the liver and the kidneys, they are as the poles of a generator that are positive and negative in their reaction. The liver is an excretory and secreting organ. The kidneys are excretory and secreting, but in the opposite way and manner. The liver prepares values for the *assimilating,* and necessary elements to produce better assimilation. The functioning of the kidneys is rather to *purify* the circulation by taking from the blood supply infectious

forces that are carried off by the slushing of same with the quantities of water taken. See?   514-4

Chakras and Life-Force Channels

Cayce's discourses include many on the body's spiritual dynamics.
He supported and developed further many of the concepts that Eastern
religions have taught for thousands of years. According to these ancient
schools, many of the body's major systems may be used for *spiritual*
activity as well as their more common physical activities. According to
Cayce's insights from his contact with the deeper, collective consciousness, the seven major endocrine glands that secrete hormones directly
into the bloodstream to keep the body running optimally are a physical portion of the seven spiritual centers that Eastern schools have been
teaching about, the chakras, which literally means "spinning wheels."
This aspect of the endocrine glands' function can effect significant
changes in the vibrations and consciousness of a mind inhabiting a
body that has enlivened chakras. The central nervous system, so vital to
living in the three-dimensional world, is also a portion of the pathway
of the life force through the body, called the "kundalini" by Eastern
schools. Moving the life force up through the spinal column nerves can
raise the vibrations and help the mind perceive beyond higher levels of
consciousness.

Much of this was known in the sacred and often secret temple schools
of ancient cultures around the world. For example, the staff carried by
the god Mercury (also known as Hermes by the Greeks, Thoth by the
Egyptians, and Enoch by the Hebrews) remains today as the emblem of
modern medicine (the caduceus). But few know its original meaning. It
is an excellent emblem for physical healing because it contains the
metaphysical structure of the body. The main shaft with the ball at the
top is symbolic of the human central nervous system, the cerebrospinal
system: brain and spinal column, with its fluid and nerves reaching
down into the body. The double serpents around this shaft symbolize
the autonomic nervous system: a woven complex of nerves and ganglia
that innervates the blood vessels, heart, muscles, viscera, and glands,
from the brain down through the body, and controls their involuntary

functions. The autonomic system is composed of a sympathetic and parasympathetic division (hence the two interwoven serpents). The wings at the top of the shaft symbolize the mind, particularly the power of the mind over the body.

An important but often forgotten teaching in several ancient temple schools addresses the movement of the life force in the body. It was taught that when the life force flows downward and outward through the body's structures, one becomes fully incarnate and conscious in this world; when the life force flows inward and upward through these same structures, then one moves beyond this reality and becomes conscious of the heavens. Many of the classical schools taught that moving this life force, or kundalini, is accomplished by using the breath. The Taoist teacher Liu Hua-yang wrote: "There is a turn upward toward Heaven when the breath is drawn in. When the breath flows out, energy is directed towards the Earth. In two intervals one gathers Sacred Energy."

Edgar Cayce's discourses affirm these energy flows and encourage us to work at entering the temple within and raising the life force in order to draw closer to the source of life, which he said is akin to electrical energy. He went so far as to say that the closest thing to God, in this world, is electrical energy.

The Body as a Temple

Eastern schools of thought are not the only source for this idea. St. Paul asked in 1 Corinthians: "Don't you know that you are a temple of God, and that the Spirit of God dwells in you?" and "Don't you know that your body is a temple of the Holy Spirit which is in you, which you have from God?" In 2 Corinthians, Paul comes right out and says it plainly: "We are a temple of the living God; even as God said, 'I will dwell in them, and walk in them; and I will be their God, and they shall be my people.'"

The disciple John hints at this when he recounts in his gospel an event when Jesus was in the great temple in Jerusalem and was asked to show the people a sign: "Jesus answered them, 'Destroy this temple, and in three days I will raise it up.' The people at the temple said, 'Forty-six years was this temple in the building, and will you raise it up in three days?' But he spoke of the temple of his body." Clearly, the disciples knew and understood the concept of the human body as a temple.

Entering the body temple, raising the energy, enlivening the spiritual centers, and uniting with the source of life was considered essential to experiencing the whole of one's true self in harmony with God–consciousness and eternal life. Moses could not ascend the mountain and meet God face to face until he first gave water to the seven maidens and raised the serpent off the desert floor—symbolic of enlivening the seven spiritual chakras and raising the kundalini energy (see further details in chapter 32).

The body's secret structure and some of the techniques to enhance the life force within us and channel it into our lives can be arranged and explained as follows.

Chakras and the Kundalini

The first formal mention of spiritual structures, including energy centers and pathways, appears in Patanjali's Yoga Sutras, ca. 300 BC. He reveals six centers and an ultimate luminescence that occurs around the top of the head. These centers are depicted in two ways: as chakras ("spinning wheels") and padmes ("lotuses"). Therefore, one may understand that the spiritual centers are both energy vortexes that generate movement as they are stimulated (as a spinning wheel) and enlightenment complexes that unfold as they grow (as an opening lotus). Edgar Cayce correlated these centers with the endocrine glandular system in the body. He also said that there are twelve, but seven are of importance here, and seven is the classic number of chakras in most ancient schools. Whenever we find seven people, places, or things in a classical story, we may correlate them with the seven spiritual centers. Cayce's most famous example of this is in his interpretation of the book of the Revelation, in which he correlates the seven churches, seals, vials, and plagues to the cleansing and opening of the seven spiritual centers within a seeker's physical body (for more on this, see my book *Edgar Cayce on the Revelation*).

Patanjali also identifies three pathways in the body. The first two are an interwoven double helix, called *ida* and *pingala*, often represented by double serpents (as in the caduceus). The third is a single path, the *sushumna*, beginning in the lower pelvic area and traveling directly up the body to the top of the head. These pathways correspond to the body's two nervous systems: the sushumna to the central nervous system, with its spinal column and the brain, and ida and pingala to the deeper autonomic nervous system, with its woven nerves that begin in the lower torso and ascend to the brain. These three pathways act as one, and the energy flows through them simultaneously.

The endocrine glands along this pathway are these, in order from lowest to highest: gonads (testes in males and ovaries in females), cells of Leydig (named after the doctor who discovered them, located in and above the gonads), adrenals (located on top of the kidneys), thymus (located in the upper chest), thyroid (in the throat), pineal (near the center of the brain at the top of the spinal fluid canal), and pituitary (just above the back of the roof of the mouth, behind the bridge of the nose, tucked under the frontal lobe). In order as chakras, they are the root, navel, solar plexus, heart, throat, crown, and brow, or third eye. Many modern books and teachers list the crown as the highest, and the third eye as sixth, but Edgar Cayce instructed us otherwise—that the kundalini energy flows up the body to the base of the brain, then over to the center of the brain and the crown of the head, and then on to the forehead and the great frontal lobe of the brain—as do many of the more classical texts and images. For example, in ancient Hinduism, the kundalini pathway is symbolized by a cobra in the striking position, not straight up. In mystical Egyptian and Mayan art, it is a winged serpent in the striking position. In Hebrew and Christian mysticism, it is the shape of the shepherd's staff. The energy flows along a path that is like a question mark (?), not like an exclamation mark (!). Pharaoh's sacred *uraeus* (from the Greek word for cobra) rises up his back, over the top of his head, and on to his forehead, at the location of the third eye.

The navel and the crown centers have a powerful magnetism between them, according to Cayce. The crown is always ready to illuminate and elevate, but individuals must open the navel center before they can begin to transcend and transform. He calls the navel center the "closed door," and the crown, the "open door." Some Eastern texts call them the "lower gate" and the "jade gate," respectively. Reconnecting these two centers is key to restoring our connection to the divine within. Here are three Cayce excerpts on this:

> This was from the flow of emotion from the kundalini center or the Lyden (Leydig) gland [navel chakra], to the ones in the center [pineal] and frontal portion of the head [pituitary]. This is nothing to be fearful of, but keep the emotions better balanced.   1523-15

> Second sight, or the super-activity of the third eye may come whenever there is the opening of the lyden (Leydig) center [navel] and the kundalini forces from same to the pineal [crown].   4087-1

> We find that there has been the opening of the Lyden (Leydig) gland, so that the kundalini forces move along the spine to the various centers that open with this attitude and these activities of the mental and spiritual forces of the body.   3421-1

Electromagnetic Qualities of the Body Temple

Several of the classical mystical concepts and images resemble electrical and electromagnetic theory and devices. Consider the caduceus, Mercury's staff: a central staff around which two serpents are wound. If the central staff was iron and the serpent coils copper, we would have the basic structure of an electromagnet. Another Egyptian artifact resembling Mercury's staff is the scepter of the goddess Isis. Over seventy of these have been found. They are composed of a single shaft around which two copper cobras coil, very similar to Mercury's staff but without the wings. The Hindu central bodily conduit of energy, the sushumna, is surrounded by the woven coils of ida and pingala.

The idea of raising one's physical and mental vibrations, one's biochemical energy, suggests the stimulation of electrons and the movement of charged particles, resulting in energy output, field generation, luminous radiation, heating effects, and other manifestations so typical of electrical and electromagnetic activity. Mystics often describe their altered experiences as generating heat, luminescence, movement, liberation, levitation, and expansion—all characteristics of electricity and magnetism. Modern–day quantum electrodynamics (QED) theorizes that electric fields are simply clouds of virtual photons and that these photons are particles that aren't even real! They come from nowhere, yet even a single–charged particle has a cloud of virtual photons around it. This virtual photon cloud is the electric field of energy and light that the mystics describe and correlate to their chakras and kundalini energy. The ancient mystics and modern physicists are sounding strangely similar.

If a meditator were to raise the energies and vibrations within his or her body, align these forces in harmony with the electrical and electromagnetic fields of the planet, then align them with the solar radiation and ultimately to the virtual fields of the universe, we could see how he could say that he had entered the infinite and felt the oneness of all life. And we would certainly expect him to feel energized and rejuvenated from the experience!

17

Ouspensky's Dimension

P.D. Ouspensky's deep philosophical "canon of thought," entitled *Tertium Organum*, was recommended by Edgar Cayce; from his trance state, he picked this book from millions. It was first published in the U.S. in 1920, and a revised edition was published the same year that Ouspensky died, 1947 (Cayce died in early 1945).

Let's spend a little time with the thoughts of one of the greatest thinkers of our time. I've chosen his ideas about consciousness.

"For some strange reason," Ouspensky muses, "men do not care to accept the answer, and they desire at all costs to receive an answer in some form that they like, refusing to recognize anything that is different from that form. They require the solution of the destiny of man as they fancy him, and they do not want to recognize that man *can and must become entirely different* [my italics]. In him there are not as yet manifest those faculties that will create his future. Man must not and cannot remain such as he is now. To think of the future of this man is just as absurd as to think of the future of a child as if it were always going to remain a child . . . Only inner growth, the unfoldment of new forces, will give to man a correct understanding of himself, his ways, his future, and give him power to organize life on earth."

In discussing higher consciousness, Ouspensky refers to the works of Edward Carpenter, a traveler and author, and Dr. R.M. Bucke, a Cana-

dian psychiatrist, both of Ouspensky's era. Carpenter traveled exten-
sively throughout the East and wrote a book titled *From Adam's Peak to
Elephanta*, in which he wrote these two paragraphs:

> The West seeks the individual consciousness—the enriched mind,
> ready perceptions and memories, individual hopes and fears, am-
> bitions, loves, conquests—*the self, the local self*, in all its phases
> and forms—and sorely doubts whether such a thing as an universal
> consciousness exists [remember, this was written in the first half of
> the 1900s, before the consciousness movement began in the latter
> half]. The East seeks the universal consciousness, and, in those cases
> where its quest succeeds, individual self and life thin away to a
> mere film, and are only the shadows cast by the glory revealed beyond.
>
> The individual consciousness is specially related to the body.
> The organs of the body are in some degrees its organs. But the
> *whole* body is only as one organ to the cosmic consciousness. To
> attain this one must have the power of knowing one's self separate
> from the body, of passing into a state of *ecstasy* in fact. Without this
> the cosmic consciousness cannot be experienced.

Many of us today have come to realize this truth. From his deep
trance state, Edgar Cayce always referred to the body as a system, an
organism that required coordination throughout in order to achieve
true health. Carpenter's idea that we can only realize this by attaining a
perspective beyond the body is true. Some of us have come to know
this directly. Deep states of dreaming, meditation, and near-death experiences have given humanity a more universal perspective of our being
and life.

Dr. Burke presents three levels of consciousness: simple, self, and cosmic. As Ouspensky so cleverly develops in his book, most animals have
one- and two-dimensional consciousness. The lower animals see the
world as a single plane, like a snail upon a surface. For the snail, the
wall in front of him is simply the same surface he has been crawling
upon but with a different gravity dynamic.

Ouspensky did not have the benefit of research done in the last half
of the 1900s. Most notable would be the work done with a mirror. Most

animals do not perceive their own reflection when placed in front of a mirror, indicating that they do not possess a clear sense of self, or self-consciousness, as Burke terms it. However, the chimpanzee (the elephant has this self-awareness as well, based on recent research) quickly perceives that the image in the mirror is not another monkey but is indeed a reflected image of himself. The chimp perceives depth and determines that the mirror is a surface and that there is no monkey behind the surface. Determining that the image is indeed his image in the mirror is another level of consciousness—self-consciousness. The chimp will begin to groom his actual body while watching the image of his body in the mirror. This is a level of perspective above simple consciousness.

Ordinary humans possess self-consciousness, but humans do not possess *cosmic* consciousness. This must be attained.

In Carpenter's view, cosmic consciousness is a level of consciousness that is beyond self, beyond the body. It is an awareness of the cosmos and one's connection with it. It is an awareness of immortality, eternal life, life beyond physical life, and therefore can only be attained beyond the mortal, temporal body and physical world.

Burke thought that cosmic consciousness would *evolve* naturally. But Ouspensky shows that it is not a product of evolution. For example, Ouspensky does not see evolution as a straight line but as occurring in distinct dimensions of life that are so perpendicular to one another that none of them naturally leads into the other. He explains that the first dimension (the snail's world) is a flat plane, but the second dimension does not exist anywhere within that plane. It is perpendicular to anything one-dimensional. The snail will never find the next dimension within the first. It would have to have an altered state of consciousness in order to perceive the second dimension—to see the wall in front of him and know that it extends perpendicular to his present surface. Therefore, first-dimensional life does not evolve into second-dimensional life. Each dimension exists within its own reality and evolves within that reality. A snail is an evolutionary wonder in the first dimension. It makes the single-celled amoeba appear primitive. Yet both are one-dimensional consciousnesses.

A cosmically conscious being would perceive the essence of the life force within and beyond the object in its field of view or, for that matter, even beyond its field of view. For example, Cayce would shut down his three-dimensional eyes in order to "see" beings many miles away from him. At a lower level of this perception, he would actually be able to describe their current three-dimensional actions ("they are praying in their bedroom"). At higher levels of perception (fifth- or sixth-dimensional levels), he would be able to "see" their past lives, future events in their current lives, even future incarnations, and their particular place within the cosmos, the infinite universe. Where was he when he saw this? That's just it, he was "nowhere." These higher dimensions are perpendicular to the spacial realities of the first three dimensions. These levels of perception do not exist within the first three dimensions. One has to break through, or beyond, 3-D perception. *When* was he? becomes an intriguing question. But he could even get beyond the "when" of perception, beyond both space and time.

Cosmic consciousness is holistic, existing beyond and within all dimensions. It is not that the mind is at some higher place or some distant place or in the past lives or future lives. It is omnipresent and omniscient. In other words, it is infinitely aware and in all places at all times. And this is not a *wiser* human. It is a *different* human, a distinct consciousness altogether. As Cayce has stated, the future body is a new "root race" body. It is not the body humanity has been using for the past 400,000 years. As St. Paul put it, "We will all be changed. In the twinkling of an eye, we will be changed."

Our outer selves will not be wiser than today but a thin film of their present dominance. This is why sensory perception will be dissimilar to the current five senses. Edgar Cayce, as a prototype, did not have an evolved sense of smell, sight, or any of the normal senses; he had perception beyond the five we currently use. He saw and heard with different eyes and ears—inner, cosmic ones. His spacial and time perceptions were beyond any enhancements of our current ones.

The human of the future will not be an evolutionary improvement of the present human but an entirely different being—a soul manifesting physically, not simply a physical person more conscious of one's soul. And, says Ouspensky, the way to this is through an inner consciousness breakthrough: the birth of the celestial self, with all its extraordinary senses.

Will there be a cosmic force that will cause this new human to be born? Or will it be a subtle, natural result of inner seeking and break-through? Cayce says that new humans will overlap with the existing ones; some will not even know what's going on. Others will be caught up in a wondrous age of enlightenment and transformation.

We who have been meditating, dreaming, changing our thought patterns, and applying alternative principles in our lives have conceived of the celestial self in the wombs of our terrestrial consciousnesses. As we continue to subdue the earthly self and yield to the birthing forces, the cosmically conscious self emerges.

18

Spirit Speaks to the Seven Centers

*I*n the vision of John the disciple in the biblical book of the Revelation, the Spirit that he sees gives a message to each of the seven churches, which Cayce correlates to seven spiritual centers within our bodies. The message to each church or spiritual center within us is in four parts. First, the Spirit will identify the spiritual center's virtue, then its weakness, then give instructions to follow, and finally, give the reward that will come from following the instructions. Here are the messages to our seven spiritual centers.

First Center—Root Chakra

Your virtue is that you have toiled and persevered, and you cannot stand evil or false spirituality. Nevertheless, you left your first love. Therefore, you must remember from where you have fallen, repent, and do the first deeds. If you overcome, I will let you eat of the Tree of Life, which is in the Paradise of God.

The Spirit reveals a great secret in its first message: We were spiritual beings first, became physical, and lost touch with our first love, the Spirit. Our instructions are to remember from where we have fallen and to reconnect with our spirituality. If we do so, we will once again eat from the tree of eternal life in the paradise of God.

The first center correlates to the Eastern root chakra. These are the sexual endocrine glands in the human body—the glands that produce life (in the female, they are the ovaries; in the male, the testes). In ancient Hindu teachings this is where the life force of the body lies, waiting to be awakened by the mind and spirit. Learning to reverse the flow of energy through this chakra by drawing the energy upward to the crown chakra, we experience the nourishment from the Tree of Life.

Second Center—Navel Chakra

To this center, the Spirit gives this message:

> I am the first and the last, who was dead and has come to life again. I know your tribulation, poverty, and slander from those claiming to be true spiritual seekers but who are of the church of Satan. Despite this, your soul is rich and you should not fear the trials and imprisonment in the body. If you cast out fear and stop doubting the truth, you will not suffer the second death, and I shall give you the crown of life.

Again, the Spirit reveals a forgotten truth: Within each of us is our spiritual self, created by God in God's image; and though that self has been dead, it will be alive again.

The key to this resurrection is to shake off our fear and stop doubting the truth. Such changes will spare us the pain of the "second death," which Cayce's readings identify with our reaching a degree of spirituality and understanding, then falling away again into selfishness and materialism. As Jesus did, Cayce instructs us to be patient and long-suffering in our spiritual growth and not let doubt tear down what we know deep within us to be true. Only by doing so may we avoid the second death.

Third Center—Solar Plexus Chakra

To this center, the Spirit gives this message:

You dwell where Satan's throne is. However, you have held fast to My name and did not deny My witness, My faithful one. Nevertheless, you have the weaknesses and vices of eating things sacrificed to idols and committing acts of immorality. This must stop. If left uncontrolled, you throw stumbling blocks in the way of spiritual growth. If you overcome, I will give you the hidden manna and I will give you a new name, etched in stone, which only you will know.

The solar plexus is one of the most powerful spiritual centers in the body. It is where the adrenals lie, ready to pump the power to fight or flee into the bloodstream. The Spirit warns us that the twin challenges of fear and anger are stumbling blocks to our spiritual growth. But the Spirit also tells us that this center has the hidden manna: it is where secret energy awaits our call. If we learn to temper the extremes of this chakra (anger and fear) and to better channel its energy, then we will receive a new name, meaning a new sense of self, who we really are.

Fourth Center—the Heart Chakra

To this center, the Spirit gives this message:

I acknowledge your charity, faith, patience, service, and works, with the recent works being greater than the former. But this I hold against you: you live life without love, seeking only gratification and pleasure. Unless you change, you will suffer great tribulation in the bed you have made for yourself. If you change your ways, however, I will give you the morning star.

"You live life without love"—an appropriate statement for the heart chakra that isn't fully awakened to its potential. Here the Spirit acknowledges our efforts to be charitable, faithful, and of service to others. But the Spirit warns us to learn to love. If we do, we will gain "the morning star," which is Venus, the light of love so worshiped by the Maya. Venus symbolizes the light of love and its creative power in our lives.

Fifth Center—the Throat Chakra

To this center, the Spirit gives this message:

> You have good deeds, you have a name, and you are alive, but you
> are closer to death than you realize. Wake up and strengthen what
> remains and you shall be clothed in white raiment, and your name
> will not be blotted out of the Book of Life, and I will confess your
> name before My Father and His angels.

Cayce's readings identify the throat chakra as the will chakra and
explain that free will is the greatest gift from God. When we engage our
free will to make choices, we are engaging an aspect of our godly nature. "Wake up!" the Spirit says, "and strengthen what remains." If we do,
we will then join the heavenly hosts and our name will be written in
the Book of Life.

Sixth Center—the Crown Chakra

The order of the chakras changes here, because Cayce says that the
energy of the kundalini life force runs up the spine to the base of the
brain, over to the center of the brain (the crown chakra), then on to the
larger frontal lobe, where the third eye opens and sees anew. Most Yoga
books will have the energy running through the third eye first, then to
the crown last. Cayce reverses these.

To this center, the Spirit gives this message:

> I give you an open door which no one can shut. I have given you a
> little power and you have kept My word and not denied My name.
> Therefore, I shall make all know that I love you. I shall keep you from
> the hour of testing, for you have kept My word of perseverance.
> Hold on to what you have and no one will take your crown. Over-
> come and I will make you a pillar in the temple of My God, and you
> will not go out from it anymore. I will write upon you the name of
> My God, and the name of the city of My God, which comes down
> from Heaven anew.

The Spirit's message to the sixth spiritual center is one of love and promise. Of all the centers, this is the only one that has no weakness or evil to overcome. It is the center where all memory is restored. As Jesus said, "When the Spirit of Truth comes, He will bring all things to your remembrance."

Seventh Center—the Third Eye

As mentioned earlier, in the Cayce arrangement, the crown chakra is the sixth spiritual center, not the seventh, as so many teach. Cayce and some ancient teachings identify the third eye as the seventh spiritual center.

To this center, the Spirit gives this message:

> You are neither cold nor hot, so because you are lukewarm, I will spit you out of My mouth. You do not see that you are wretched, miserable, poor, blind, and naked. I advise you to get truth forged in the fires of the spirit, white garments of purity so your nakedness will be clothed, and eye salve to anoint your eyes to see the real truth. Those whom I love, I reprove and discipline. If you overcome, I will give you permission to sit down with Me on My throne, as I overcame just the same, and we shall sit down with My Father on His throne.

We have arrived at the seventh spiritual center and the seventh church. The Spirit is upset because this most powerful center is lukewarm about spiritual growth and enlightenment. It warns that we don't fully comprehend just how wretched we are, despite all our material possessions. The Spirit calls us to get hot, to start working on our spiritual enlightenment and soul growth. Notice that the Spirit does not give this spiritual center a virtue—that is because it has not been awakened fully to realize its powerful blessing and gift.

How Do We Use This Information?

As in the opening Cayce reading, we can use this knowledge as an opportunity to better understand ourselves. If we go through each of our spiritual centers, understanding its virtue and its weakness, taking hold of the Spirit's instructions for improvement, we will ultimately realize the rewards promised by the Spirit. We will awaken to our true nature and our true, eternal life with the Spirit.

Sit quietly, and as you read the Spirit's messages to each spiritual center within your body, *feel* the message in and around that center. Cayce also gave the color and sound for each spiritual center. We can use these to help us generate a new level of life and vitality in our spiritual centers. See and feel the power of each color and each sound as we read and contemplate that center's virtues, weaknesses, instructions, and reward. The colors go according to the spectrum of white light when broken into its seven visible parts: red, orange, yellow, green, blue, indigo, and violet. The sounds go according to the Western musical scale: *do, re, me, fa, sol, la,* and *ti.*

In this strange collection of esoteric insights from Edgar Cayce's deep attunement to the Universal Consciousness, we find classical training in the mystical arts of illumination and transformation. It blends mystical, self-help concepts from the mysterious book of the Revelation with Eastern concepts concerning spiritual centers within our bodies. Try it for yourself. See if it finds a place in your practices. It is certainly a unique approach to spiritual enlightenment and mental transcendence.

19

Heavenly Consciousness

*W*hen asked to comment on heavenly consciousness while living in a physical life, Edgar Cayce began his psychic reply using the trinity as a model for our ideal condition. He explained that since we are in a three–dimensional world, we should know that body, mind, and soul are "the shadows" of that *from which* we have emanated and toward which we should *grow*. Somewhat surprisingly, we are actually designed to live in the world while conscious of the heavens, but we need to grow to this awareness.

As individuals do not *go* to heaven or paradise or the universal consciousness, they must *grow* to it through "applying of their abilities towards that consciousness using the virtues, the 'fruits of the spirit,'" which awaken us to the spirit and the consciousness of heaven. (2505–1)

As we analyze ourselves, we find ourselves body, mind, and soul with a three–dimensional consciousness. The reading explains that this is already a perfect design for relating to earth life and heavenly life. The readings say that God "in power and might has three phases of expression: spirit, or soul; mind; and body—Father, Son, and Holy Spirit." (2800–2) Yet, Cayce explained, these are one, as they are with each of us. Cayce asked us: "How could He be in heaven, in earth, in this place or that place, and be aware of an individual and at the same moment or time be aware of a presence in places miles away?" He answered: Be–

cause "there is no time, no space in the Unity of the at-onement. This you know. This you often have a consciousness of, yet not a full awareness. You crystallize, you demonstrate, you make an at-onement by your own attunement to His conscious presence that becomes a reality in material expressions as Creative Forces can, do, and are in those who are of one mind, one purpose, one intent, one desire." (1158-9)

From Cayce's perspective, our mind is the bridge between this world, this reality, and the heavenly one. Mind can link body to spirit, personality to universal consciousness. The mind does this by practicing the fruits of the spirit while in physical life—thereby spiritualizing the physical. The fruits of the spirit are love, kindness, understanding, forgiveness, patience, and the like—not only in our daily actions, but also in our daily thoughts. Then we need the at-onement consciousness, which the readings say begins with becoming aware of God's presence with us and with those around us, despite outward appearances of separation, isolation, and individuality. All exist in this unity, whether they are conscious of it or not. As we become conscious of it, we *grow* toward a heavenly consciousness.

Time in meditation is one of the best ways to reconnect with this at-onement with Life itself and the unseen reality of oneness.

Of course, we have to grow to this awareness. It doesn't just come upon us and boom, we're enlightened. Though there may be spontaneous moments of illumination along the way, the way unfolds as we apply ourselves. Enlightenment and understanding come from *doing*, not just from thinking or believing. In the "doing," the readings say, "comes the understanding." But doing from a centered place of oneness is the best way, and periods in meditation help us realize this.

Here's an interesting reading that shines some more light on our topic:

Q: When and where will I next incarnate and will I be associated with people in present incarnation and whom?
A: Better get into shape so that you can incarnate. That depends a great deal upon what one does about the present opportunities. It isn't set for time immemorial as to be what you will be from one experience to the other. For, as has been given, there are unchange-

able laws. The Creator intended man to be a companion with Him. Whether in heaven or in the earth or in whatever consciousness, the created was intended to be a companion with the Creator. How many incarnations will it require for you to be able to be a companion with the Creative Forces wherever you are?

That is also a law. What you sow, ye reap. What is, then, that which is making for the closer association of body, mind, and soul to Father, Son, and Holy Spirit? He that heeds not, then, has rejected, and there is the need for remembering the unchangeable law: "Though He were the Son, yet learned He obedience through the things which He suffered." Are you to be greater than your Lord? Where will these occur? Where do you make them? The place where you are, is the place to begin. What were the admonitions? "Use that you have in hand. Today, will you (if you will) hear His voice, harden not your heart."   416-18

And another reading:

There has also come a teacher who was bold enough to declare himself as the son of the living God. He set no rules of appetite. He set no rules of ethics, other than "As ye would that men should do to you, do you even so to them," and to know "Inasmuch as you do it unto the least of these, your brethren, you do it unto your Maker." He declared that the kingdom of heaven is within each individual entity's consciousness, to be attained, to be aware of, through meditating upon the fact that God is the Father of every soul.

Jesus, the Christ, is the mediator. And in Him, and in the study of His examples in the earth, is *Life*— and that you may have it more abundantly. He came to demonstrate, to manifest, to give life and light to all.

Here, then, you find a friend, a brother, a companion. As He gave, "I call you not servants, but brethren." For, as many as believe, to them He gives power to become the children of God, the Father; joint heirs with this Jesus, the Christ, in the knowledge and in the awareness of this presence abiding ever with those who set this ideal before them.   357-13

And another inspiring reading:

In the manner, then, to aid most, raise in self that beauty of spirit as expressed in Him: "Suffer little children to come unto me, for of such is the kingdom of heaven." In raising, then, the consciousness of self that kingdom is being manifested, expressed, in the body. Though not seen or understood by us, there is *His* will being accomplished, that this entity may be one with Him in that kingdom. Raise that as oft as seems well with you, and these will bring it about, for "thoughts *are* deeds," and as their currents run there are created those forces that make for the closer affinity.   281-7

Cayce also gave a little prayerful affirmation that we may say throughout the day to help us keep centered and awakened to the Spirit, to the Oneness, and its presence within us:

"Our Father, our God. Let the heaven of consciousness of the presence of the Christ light my pathway of choice, that I may choose in this life to be that for which your purposes brought me into being—now." (281-7)

20

Getting Guidance

Many of us on this path need and seek guidance from alternative sources. Among these sources are psychic readings, hypnotic sessions, dream quests, intuitive perceptions, and meditative revelations. Some of us use the Scriptures and Cayce readings as our *vade mecum*, our guiding reference compendiums. Some consult the stars. Some toss lots or runes or engage the I Ching or Tarot cards. Some use all of these sources and more.

These alternative sources or devices can and have worked for humans throughout the ages. In some well-publicized moments, God has spoken directly to humans, giving insight and direction. Hearing messages from "God" ("God told me to do it") has often ended in evil acts and jail time! And "hearing voices" is not commonly a positive sign (see the Appendix for a Q and A on this topic). However, the Cayce readings say that God still speaks to those who will listen (see chapter 24, "Talking with God"), but the hearers don't become insane or antisocial.

Let's explore alternative sources for guidance for life situations and personal decisions. We can group these sources into two major categories: those that consult others and those that access the inner self. The most popular are those that consult others: psychics, mediums, hypnotherapists, astrologers, card readers, palm readers, and the like. All of these assume an unusual ability on the part of someone else. We simply have to show up, pay the fee, and receive the information. In some cases, the guidance is correct and useful. In some cases, it is spectacular and affects us and our lives in distractive ways, leading us off in directions we never really wanted to go but felt directed to do, often to the detriment of our families, friends, and our own lives. In some cases, the guidance is ambiguous, causing us to never feel that we correctly understood it. I have interviewed people who received Cayce readings but felt they really didn't understand them at first.

Without question, there are people who manifest special abilities to "read" the Akashic records, cards, stars, and souls. The problem is finding them, or finding the right one for you and your needs. Some readers are quite good with health situations but not with past lives. Some are good with past lives but not with coming circumstances in one's life. Some can see very well your situation and future opportunities or dangers but not your body's condition. Few are good at reading all of the influences affecting a person today. As you may know, the A.R.E. maintains a list of psychics, as a service to those interested. In your local area there are astrologers, card and palm readers, and others who may be able to help you get some insight. Most can be chosen by their reputation; asking others who already spent the money and got the advice is the best way to determine if the reader is worth a try.

Even if you do find a good reader for you, the real work begins after the reading, when you have to apply the guidance in your life! Of course, this is the challenge with any guidance, isn't it? I once interviewed a person who received guidance from Edgar Cayce himself (something I'm sure all of us would have wanted). He told me that the work involved in what Cayce told him to do was too much. He wasn't willing to do it. But I've also interviewed people who did do all the work that Cayce directed them to do, yet felt like they never really got the result they were expecting. Of course, there were many who did grasp the guidance in their Cayce readings and gained much from applying them in their lives.

Getting information is the easy part. Making it work for you is another matter altogether! Often, Cayce would only give a little direction in the first readings for people, keeping more for later, after they had applied some of the initial guidance. He often said that all change is to be achieved one step at a time, here a little there a little, and that long-suffering and patience are required for significant achievement along the path.

Inner guidance is even more difficult than outer because it requires that one develop one's own skills at reading before even getting the reading! But, according to Cayce, the inner methods have the added benefit of developing one's soul in the process of getting help. Cayce says that the senses necessary for alternative guidance are the natural senses of our soul. Our body's senses are sight, hearing, smell, touch, and taste. Our soul's senses are clairvoyance (seeing beyond the present location and time), clairaudience (hearing beyond the vibrating of the physical ear drums; "He who has ears to hear, let him hear what the spirit says"), and clairsentience (perceiving by means beyond the physical senses, especially by feeling). "Clair" is a prefix derived from the French word *clair*, meaning "clear," as in clear-seeing or clear-hearing. The word *psycho*, a prefix in some of the compound words used to explain these soul powers, such as *psychokinesis*, is derived from the Greek word *psyché*, meaning "breath, spirit, mind," as in perceiving with the mind or the spirit rather than the body's senses.

As many of you know, Cayce was specifically asked how individuals could become more psychic. His answer became the "Search for God" material, containing such topics as: "Spirit," "Patience," "Cooperation," "Destiny of the Mind," "The Lord Thy God is One," and so on. Much of this material can be distilled into two basic concepts: (1) extrasensory abilities come from being in greater proximity to one's psyché or soul, which naturally has these as its senses; and (2) the more completely one's self is set aside, and the deeper soul self is made at one with the Universal Consciousness, with God, then the clearer and more accurate the guidance. Obviously, this is going to take some effort and time to develop.

The methods Cayce recommended most are meditation and dream study. Dreams happen naturally and, according to Cayce, are the safest way to awaken our psychic ability. Meditation is similar to entering the dimensions of sleep and dreaming but is done while in a semi-wakeful state. Another technique promoted through Cayce's at-onement with the Universal Consciousness is "creative writing." He described this as sitting quietly and in a reflective state, even a spiritually attuned state, and then letting thoughts and ideas flow, writing them down as they come. Don't think of these as being for others or for publication. The guidance is for you; it is communication from your higher self, even from God, to your outer self.

We all need guidance. Life at this level is often unclear. There are others who can help us. There are latent abilities within us that can help. Some skills will need to be developed, but they are not beyond learning. The hardest part of getting guidance is applying it. And, according to Cayce, guidance or knowledge that is not applied becomes "sin." To know to do something and not to do it is unhealthy, in this lifetime and the next. So take a deep breath, get up, and get searching for that important insight into your circumstances and potential. It has been promised: "Seek, and you will find. Ask, and it will be given you. Knock, and the door will be opened." But once it is, you have to do your part by using the breakthrough in daily life, step by step, little by little. Go for it now.

Dangers with Guidance

Those of us on a path of enlightenment and guidance that comes from within, from one's soul and one's Maker, must be aware of the dangers involved and develop ways to avoid tragic mistakes in understanding and interpretation.

Guidance from our higher selves and God passes through a whirlwind of personal dynamics that can distort the true meaning of any message. Since the language of deeper consciousness is often imagery, metaphor, and symbolism, we are vulnerable to misinterpreting the message. Inner thoughts can become mixed with earthly impulses and urges. Impressions made upon our subconscious by the teachings and examples of others can affect our perspective without our even knowing it. As we move more toward living the spirit of the law rather than the letter of the law, we are increasingly susceptible to mistakes—from the harmless to the extremely harmful.

It is one thing to misinterpret our mother's death in a dream but quite another thing to hear God guiding us to divorce our spouse, quit our job, or kill another person.

Several years ago the Mormon Church went through another deadly experience with "divine guidance," leading to the murder of one of its twenty-four-year-old members and her fifteen-month-old baby. The killers, her brothers-in-law (and the uncles of her child), felt that they were "guided by the hand of God."

Mormons believe in divine revelation for each person, that God does guide individual souls from within. But after too many of these types of crimes, the Mormon Church has developed a qualifier that perhaps we should seriously consider: God does not guide anyone to break the laws of God as set down in the Bible, specifically the Ten Commandments. One of those laws is "Thou shalt not kill."

Many churches and communities have experienced the shock and sadness of misunderstood divine guidance, of high-flying spirituality that crashes under the weight of human nature. As the Mormons have had to do, let's take some time here to consider how we may avoid the dangers of inner guidance.

In *The Secret of the Golden Flower*, master Lü-tsu teaches that "all changes of spiritual consciousness depend upon the heart." He explains that the right way is only one wing of the sacred bird, the other wing is the right heart; and the bird doesn't fly with one wing. He says, "There is a secret charm which, although it works very accurately, is yet so fluid that it needs extreme intelligence and clarity, and the most complete absorption and tranquillity."

One cannot approach the higher levels of spirituality and consciousness without weighing one's heart as one goes along. One needs to use all of one's intellectual faculties to make sure one has the clarity, absorption, and tranquillity necessary to detect distorting influences and comprehend the true intent and meaning of inner guidance.

The ancient Egyptians had a similar process. Their papyrus drawings show them weighing hearts against the feather of truth. The feather symbolizes the delicacy of the truth. A heart that is heavy with self-centered longings, unfinished business, or regrets keeps the mind from lifting high enough to get a clear view of the better self's perspective. Guidance is then viewed through the lower self's perspective only.

Jesus taught us to judge by "the fruits" of our actions, thoughts, and words. Do they bring good fruit that nourishes or poison fruit that kills the Snow White within each of us. Of course, it is always best to determine what fruits may come *before* planting the seeds. We need to guard against negative thought seeds and habitual thought patterns that create an unhealthy atmosphere for good fruit.

Perhaps the number one lesson Jesus gave was love. The spirit of love is the best atmosphere for the heart to bear good fruit. The Cayce readings expand this with the statement: God is law, and the law is love.

If these two Mormon men, mentioned earlier, had nourished their hearts in the open air of love rather than the fog of fear of the law, they would not have killed their niece and sister-in-law, no matter what they saw as her errors. As Jesus said to the lawbreaking woman, "Neither do I condemn thee. Go thy way and sin no more." When Peter asked how often we should forgive our fellow humans, sighting seven times as the acceptable amount in those days, Jesus replied, "Seventy times seven!"

From his deep attunement to the Universal Consciousness, Edgar Cayce explained that perceiving inner information is comparable to viewing a stick in water, which appears bent but is not (900-59). The distortion is a natural complexity of the medium through which the message is being viewed. He states that the best way to be sure that we are viewing the information correctly is "through the powers of the Holy One, by the Creator, [and] the wholesome, the more righteous life, or the more righteous *use* of life." (276-6) In other words, using life for the right purposes in conjunction with regular attunement to the Holy One, the Creator, helps us see more clearly. He encourages us to take time to review and understand our purposes and ideals. Are we self-centered, self-righteous, or do we seek to make life better for those around us, to make the world a better place for us having lived in it, like George Bailey did in the movie *It's a Wonderful Life*.

Here is Cayce's reading about distorting guidance (I've edited it for clarity and to focus on the point):

> Q: Explain: "By the suggestion the subconscious may be wavered by the forces that are brought to bear on the subconscious to reach conscious mind." [The questioner is referring to reading 3744-3, par. 18-A.]

A: In the wavering of forces from the subconscious to the conscious mind, first we must take into consideration that conscious mind is of the material world. The subconscious mind may only be fully understood when viewed from the spiritual viewpoint. The conscious mind rarely gains the entrance to truth in the subconscious, save in rest, sleep, or when such consciousnesses are subjugated through the act of the individual, as in the case of Edgar Cayce [during a reading]. The illustration is, a stick in water appears bent. When the consciousness views subconscious forces they appear wavered or bent, when viewed from wholly a material viewpoint, whether from the dream in sleep, or viewed by a conscious mind or material mind from trance or from the subconscious condition. Hence in the sleep we may have the superseding of the consciousness and thus waver the appearance of truth obtained, or we may have the suggestion as is given to a mind [like Cayce's when in trance] directing the truth to be obtained from subconscious forces bent in such a manner as to give the wavered aspect to the truth. In such a manner, or in one of such manners, then do we see the wavering often (not always) of truths obtained by a consciousness from the subconscious forces.   (Based on 900-59)

Our material minds can bend the truth coming from the subconscious and superconscious levels. The bending is due to our perspective being too material, too literal, or from a predisposition to certain aspects of truth as we see it or expect it—in other words, the "suggestions" given to ourselves by ourselves and others prior to getting guidance from within. Thus we set ourselves up for misinterpretations, misunderstandings.

Few things will give us more hope for true inner guidance than building a clear, enlivened mind and a pure heart.

Here are two affirmations Cayce suggested we use to help us develop these keys:

Create in me a pure heart and renew a righteous spirit within me, cleansing my life, my heart, my body, through the love in the Christ life.   281-20

Create within me a perfect mind, O God! With the desire and the purpose to use my life, my talents, my gifts, in Thy Service! Let my going in, my coming out, be acceptable in Thy sight. And as I meditate, be thou nigh unto me.   308-6

21

Importance of Metaphor

*E*dgar Cayce once interpreted a dream about finding gold on the back acres of the dreamer's land to mean that she should search for the gold that is never stolen, never lost in the back acres of her heart and mind. Amazingly, this particular dreamer, while acknowledging the wisdom of Cayce's interpretation, still wanted to know if there was also real gold on her property. He replied that "real gold" is the everlasting gold in the heart and mind, not metal that can only be used while incarnate.

The predominance of our physical life and nature causes us to consider the physical as the "real" rather than the thought or spirit of something. These we consider to be "imaginary" treasures. Consider this Psalm.

Psalm 36:7–9
How precious is thy steadfast love, O God! The children of men take refuge in the shadow of thy wings. They feast on the abundance of thy inner place, and thou givest them drink from the river of thy delights. For within thee is the fountain of life; in thy light do we see light.

Here we have a psalm with mystical and metaphysical language, not literal, physical language: "the shadow of thy wings," "the abundance of thy inner place," "the rivers of thy delights," "within thee is the fountain of life," and "in thy light do we see light." The effect upon our minds as we open to the metaphysical implications of these words is buoyant, uplifting, expansive. Using actions that normally bring vital, physical gratification—"take refuge," "feast," "drink," "see"—the inspired poet leads us beyond the physical to "the shadow of thy wings," "the abundance of thy inner place," "the river of thy delights," and "thy light."

Let's take this a step further. What is a piece of bread? It is a nourishing food for our bodies, right? Right! But what, then, does Jesus mean when he says to his disciples, "I have bread that you do not know about." Upon hearing this, the statement puzzles them. They ask, among themselves, who brought Jesus some bread. None of them did! Jesus is not talking about physical bread; he is using *bread*, a nourishing food, as a metaphor for a source of nourishment that we do not know about. The psalmist is using *refuge*, *feast*, and *drink* as metaphors for a refuge, feast, and drink that we don't take seriously enough. The ultimate source of nourishment and comfort is not in physical food or refuge but in the Spirit that gives these their nourishment and comfort. The life–giving ingredient in bread comes from a source beyond the grain. That is the real source for all nourishment. And as we have all come to know, we can lift ourselves into that Spirit that gives life all physical matter, and in so doing we have direct access to nourishment, to a bread that too few know about or use.

Try experiencing the *meta*physical gifts from God: the shadow of his wings, the abundance of his inner place, the river of his delights, and his light. Let's seek it, ask for it, knock on the doors of our hearts and minds for it. We have been promised that if we seek, we will find. We simply have to get over our totally physical sense of reality. We have to seek beyond the physical. Cayce encourages us to "use the imaginative forces." Imagine (using that power of the mind) the Life Force being available to you for nourishment, comfort, and guidance. Then act on that imaginative force by lifting your heart and mind into that non–physical contact with Life's Source. Let it flow into you and through you to others throughout the day. You'll have bread that others will want to discover.

How precious is thy steadfast love, O God! The children of men take refuge in the shadow of thy wings. They feast on the abundance of thy inner place, and thou givest them drink from the river of thy delights. For within thee is the fountain of life; in thy light do we see light.

22

In the Presence

*H*igh on a list of activities for improving ourselves spiritually, mentally, and even physically ought to be time spent in the presence of the "Creator of the universe and all the forces and powers therein," as Cayce once referred to God. Yet, life being what it is in this world, time in the Presence is often at the bottom of our list. In many cases, we acknowledge the importance of being in the Presence but don't make the time for it. Some of us believe that it isn't even possible. But there's more to the low priority of being in the Presence than busyness and doubts. Cayce once observed that even those who have experienced the Presence don't always return to it but get lost in the many activities of life and individual consciousness. Cayce says that *some* of this is due to "the lack of what may be called stamina, faith, patience or what not."

But what is it about human consciousness and life that causes us to live barely conscious of God? Is it that proverbial apple that distracts us from all of the other joys and wonders of walking with God in the Garden? The apple of Genesis was on the Tree of the Knowledge of Good and Evil. Why would we be forbidden to eat from that tree? It would seem that knowledge would be helpful to our development. Cayce says that the ultimate goal of every soul is to know itself to be itself, yet one with the Whole. Therefore, self is good. It is to be developed, fully known, and then united with the Whole. Did forbidding us

from eating of the Tree of the Knowledge of Good and Evil have something to do with our current difficulty with living in the Presence?

The answer is spiritual and physical, and somewhat complex; but
let's explore it. According to Cayce, the fall from full consciousness of
God occurred long before physical life. It occurred in the spirit and the
mind, before our souls began to incarnate. This is indicated in the first
chapters of Genesis.

In the first two chapters, God creates us *three* times! The author of
Genesis cleverly conveys this story, even changing the name of God to
indicate our shifting relationship with Him/Her.

The first creation is expressed in those well-known words, "Let there
be light." Cayce explains that this light was the Logos, the Christ, with
which the disciple John opened his Gospel: "In the beginning was the
Word, and the Word was with God and the Word was God." In the
original Greek manuscript, the word for "Word" was the Greek word
"Logos," which means much more than *word*. The Logos is defined by
philosophers and theologians as the rational principle that governs and
develops the universe and which incarnated in Jesus Christ, as the disciple indicated when he wrote, "And it became flesh and dwelt among
us." We were part of the Logos. Cayce explains: "In the beginning, God
said, 'Let there be light.' You are one of those sparks of light, with all the
ability of Creation, with all the knowledge of God." This first creation is
our spiritual, godly being. Again, as the psalmist writes: "You are gods,
sons [and daughters] of the Most High," Psalm 82:6.

The second creation occurs later, in verse 26 of chapter one of Genesis, where "Elohim" creates us in "their" image. Elohim is a plural Hebrew word that English Bibles translate as "God." Many scholars have
wrestled with the question of why a plural word was chosen for the
name of the Creator. One answer is that the original and most high God
was and is all-inclusive, collective, not separate from any of the creation, and that created beings are intrinsic portions of the Whole. Cayce
stated it this way, "Not only God is God, for self is a part of that Oneness." The Whole, however, is greater than the sum of its parts.

The Genesis author writes: "Let *us* make adam [English Bibles use the
word *man* here, but it is actually the Hebrew word *adam*, meaning "a
being"] in *our* image, after *our* likeness" [italics mine]. This is the second

creation. It is the creation of our individual soul, mind, and free will.

It's important to note that this being was also created male and fe-male in one, and the gender characteristics were not separated until chapter 2, verse 21. This is the original, hermaphroditic nature of our complete soul, as Cayce and others have taught.

The third creation came after we had begun to move away from oneness with Elohim. The author conveys this by changing the name of God to Yahweh Elohim, which English Bibles translate as "Lord God." The au-thor writes: "Then the Lord God formed adam [the being] of dust from the ground [now we are beginning to incarnate into matter], and breathed into his nostrils the breath of life; and adam became a living being."

Cayce indicates that coming to the third dimension and the physical world was a further movement away from conscious contact with the infinite Whole, a process that had already begun in the spirit and the mind as we developed individual consciousness. Our self-motivated desires, combined with the power of free will, led us to seek life inde-pendent of the original at-onement we had with God and the rest of creation. This eventually led to a physical body. A physical body was the ultimate in separation and isolation, confining our free, universal, infinite mind and spirit to an encasement. Nevertheless, the Lord God attempted to help us with this, even though He/She knew it was not ideal. Allowing free will to be truly free was more important than keep-ing us on track. Free will, no matter how many mistakes were made with it, was the key to true companionship with God.

It is important to note that at this point in the story, the Lord God also creates the Garden and the Tree of the Knowledge of Good and Evil, placing it in the middle of the Garden and asking adam [the being] not to eat from it, lest he/she die. This indicates that, though we were now physically confined in matter, we remained *immortal*.

Here the Lord God notes that it is not good that we are alone. Yet, after searching the whole earth for suitable physical companions for us and finding none, the Lord God decides to create a natural companion from within our original nature. To do this, the Lord God causes a deep sleep to fall upon adam [the being] and separates *ishshah* [female] and *ish* [male]. From here on, there are now two bodies, one for the female half of our original nature, and the other for the male half.

It is unfortunate that the male portion of adam [the being] received the name Adam. If he had been named something like Bob, it would have helped us through the ages to better understand the truth about the genders. It would have also helped if English Bibles had used the word *side* instead of *rib*. The same Hebrew word has both meanings. Truly, Eve was taken from a *side* of the original being, not a rib.

In the Garden was the most cunning beast of all, the serpent. Fascinatingly, the Hebrew word used for this creature comes from a root word meaning "the sound of a whisper," as in a hiss (*naw-khash*). But it also has the connotation of conjuring a magic spell by whispering, as an enchanter would do. Add to this, Cayce's correlating the serpent with the mind—the whispering mind of individual consciousness with free will—and we have a better sense of just how much a part of ourselves this cunning creature was and is today.

On a physical level, the serpent also represents our kundalini energy. Lowering our consciousnesses and energy, in order to better experience this physical plane and matter, compares with the serpent coming down out of the tree to crawl on the ground. This is why so many mystical teachings talk about "raising the serpent" in order to better experience God's presence. Jesus taught Nicodemus three "heavenly" concepts: (1) No one ascends to heaven but he or she who already descended from it; (2) We have been physically born, but now we must be born again, giving birth to our spiritual self; and (3) As Moses raised the serpent in the desert, so must the Son of Man [the Daughter of Man] be raised up to eternal life. Moses raises the serpent following God's instructions and prior to his ability to ascend the mount to meet God face-to-face. Raising the serpent is raising the mind's consciousness and body's energies in order to operate at high levels of vibrations, levels that are more compatible with God's.

Cayce said the winged serpent in ancient Egyptian and Mayan teachings reflected this very process. The Mayan's great god Kukulcan (Quetzalcoatl, for the Aztecs) was their winged serpent savior. One might think of the wings as the rising consciousness and the serpent as the rising kundalini energy.

All of this is in pursuit of an answer to our question: Why forbid us from eating of the Tree of Knowledge? Here is Cayce's clarifying answer:

When an entity, a soul, uses a period of manifestation—in whatever realm of consciousness—to its own indulgencies, then there is need for the lesson, or for the soul understanding . . . to become aware of the error of its way. What, then, was the first cause of this awareness? It was the eating, the partaking, of knowledge; knowledge without wisdom—or that as might bring pleasure, satisfaction, gratifying—not of the soul but of the phases of expression in that realm in which the manifestation was given. Thus in the three-dimensional phases of consciousness such manifestations become as pleasing to the eye [apple's beauty], pleasant to the body appetites [apple's taste]. Thus the interpretation of the experience of deviation from the divine law is given in the form as of eating of the tree of knowledge. Who, what influence, caused this—you ask? It was that influence which had set itself in opposition to the soul remaining in that state of at-onement [with the Whole, with God].

                                                                                                815-7

With the loss of at-onement, the sacred Tree of Life was then guarded from us as an act of Divine mercy so that we could not live forever in this state of separation. Death occurs for the first time. We were and are celestial beings, children of the most high God, universal, infinite, eternal. We could not be allowed to live forever in the individual, finite, temporal world of matter.

It is helpful to know that Cayce said the fundamental basis of all sin or evil is self for self's sake. The earth, the flesh, and individuality are not evil in and of themselves. It is how we use them that makes for the darkness of sinfulness and evil or the lightness of virtue and good. But it is equally important to note Cayce's emphasis on at-onement with God. How many of us are in that state? Can we consciously know at-onement with the Infinite, Universal Creator? Can a finite mind be one with the Infinite One?

The answer found in all mystical branches of the great religions of the world is yes. A finite being can indeed experience the Infinite, as did Enoch, Moses, Elijah, and many others, including Buddha and Muhammad.

However, experiencing the Infinite One is not as difficult as *maintain-*

ing oneness with It. Most humans have had a sense of the Presence of God from time to time in their lives. The challenge is budgeting time for experiencing the Presence, then coming out into daily life and sustaining a sense of at–onement with the Presence as we speak, act, think, and engage with others. It is subtle, gentle, and natural, once one becomes familiar with It.

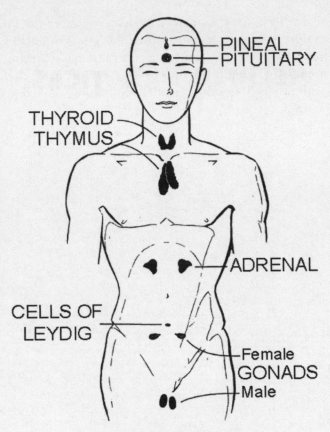

PINEAL
PITUITARY

THYROID
THYMUS

ADRENAL

CELLS OF
LEYDIG

Female
GONADS
Male

Endocrine Glands

Section Four

HELPFUL PRACTICES

23

Journaling

*A*s amazing as it may sound, medical science has found that patients who write down their feelings and memories in a journal actually recover better from illnesses and have better general health than their counterparts who do not (reported in the *Journal of the American Medical Association*). *Newsweek* magazine reported: "Researchers found that asthma patients who wrote about experiences such as car accidents, physical abuse, divorce or sexuality improved their lung function by 19 percent on average. And in patients with rheumatoid arthritis, symptoms decreased by 28 percent." These are impressive facts.

Journaling is good for our health; and not just physical health, but mental too. "Think of journaling as a pocket-therapist," says Eldonna Bouton, author of *Loose Ends: A Journaling Tool for Tying up the Incomplete Details of your Life and Heart*. "If you take the time to write out your thoughts you will find that you are much calmer than when you started. And often, the answer to a problem is as close as your favorite pen." In a world where Prozac is a household word, people are searching for alternative ways to combat depression and anxiety. Many are finding that journaling is a successful form of therapy and often as cathartic as talking to a professional.

In addition to its healthful benefits, journaling is an excellent way to self-discovery. Edgar Cayce was asked about this: "Q: Would you sug-

gest I keep a daily diary? A: It's good for everyone, to look at self occasionally. Hence as has been given, *know* thyself, in *whom* thou believest!
Not of earthly, not of material things, but mental and spiritual and *why*!
And by keeping a record of self—not as a diary, but thy purposes, what
you have thought, what you have desired, the good that you have done.
This will bring physical and mental reactions that will be in keeping
with the purposes for which each soul enters a material manifestation."
(830–3) Obviously, we are not talking about keeping one of those day-
by–day diaries of what we did. This type of diary is an expression of our
deeper feelings, beliefs, and ideals. It is a means to discovering who we
really are and what we really seek out of life.

But there is an even greater benefit to journaling, something Cayce
called "creative" or "inspirational" writing. He described it as an enlightened form of automatic writing, which he discouraged. In inspirational
writing, you seek to attune your earthly, everyday self to your higher
self and the Universal Consciousness and then write the insights, guidance, or whatever comes to you. It differs from automatic writing in
that you actually want to avoid mindless influences. You want the
Source of all life, God, and the part of you that was made in God's
image.

In one reading, Cayce gave a detailed procedure for successfully
channeling inspired writing from deep within yourself and from the
Universal Consciousness:

1. It would be well that an hour be chosen for such activities when
there is quiet and when the mental and material body may become
perfectly relaxed. Such periods should be chosen as an exact period.
Say, as an illustration, 10:00 to 10:30 in the evening. Enter then in this
silence, each evening, at this specific time.

2. Enter into the silence with some form of rote that is rather in the
form of a prayer or as an affirmation to the inner self, that the forces or
powers that may manifest through self at such a period may ever mag-
nify the presence of not only constructive influence, but from the throne
of grace and mercy itself [see the affirmation below that Cayce recom-
mended].

3. Sit with a subdued or shaded light, with paper, pencil, or materi-
als before self at a desk or table [or computer word processor].

4. What is given or is an *impelling* influence that causes you to write, then *write*! Do not reread but put it away at least until it is given from within to review or to go over that which has been given.

We will find, this is as being of the intuitive or psychic influences from within self; but impelled by that of the higher influence, higher force that may manifest into individuals' experience that seek His face. And this closes self to those influences that may interrupt or cause their own individual expression.

> Do not grow weary if in turns with self nothing comes for perhaps days, or that much is given at one period in the beginning and little or nothing later. Be true to self, not to read nor have read that written, until it is *given* thee to do so. 282-5

Here's a prayer or affirmation that Cayce gave for this very purpose:

> Q: Give me an affirmation that will bring the highest forces.
> A: Father, as I surround myself with the consciousness of the Christ Spirit, wilt Thou be the guide. Send Thou, O God, that influence into my mind, my heart, my soul, my body, that will make and create the best in me, that I may use the attributes of my mind, my soul, my body, for Thy glorification. 317-7

That's a powerful prayer! You can see how surrounding yourself with these words and imagining their full meaning coming upon yourself would bring only the highest and the best influence.

Now, we don't all have to seek creative, inspirational writing. Any work with journaling is going to help us. Get yourself a special journal or notebook, or create a file in your word processor, and begin writing your feelings, thoughts, ideals, or whatever moves you. Use this time to gain insight into personal problems or life issues.

I sit at my computer, get into a meditative state, and then write my feelings. I try to identify issues that are most important. I explore elements of the issues and my feelings as well as the feelings of others involved. Then I list my options. If the options seem limited, then I begin an anything–goes listing of "What if . . . " ideas, to see if I can discover a new option. Sometimes no solutions present themselves, but the processing makes me clearer about the situation and the feelings involved. Frequently, after journaling on some difficult problems, I find that days or weeks later a solution or opportunity to adjust the circumstances presents itself. I believe that the journaling puts the issues into motion in the subliminal realms of life, and this eventually manifests a solution in the outer life.

Combining one's dream journaling with one's regular journaling is very helpful. Often the themes in the dreams correlate with the problems or ideas expressed in the journaling. I also find that this type of inner work ebbs and flows. Sometimes I'm really into the inner processing and discovery and spend a lot of time writing and recording dreams. Other times, I'm really involved in living life and engaging in the activities of each day. This cycles back and forth, as does life.

24

Talking with God

*T*alking with God sounds like something that happened in biblical days. Today, if you said you've been talking with God, you're likely to be considered a potential mass murderer who may pop any day, and we'll all see you on TV being carried away by the authorities. But from Edgar Cayce's attunement to the Collective Consciousness, he taught that God still speaks with those who seek Him/Her: "God speaks directly to each of you—even as He has promised," (440-4); "Even under stress, He goes *with* you—*all* the way. For as He has given, 'If you will but ask, I will *come*, I will *abide*, I will be with you!'" (622-6); and "Is not the better way to talk it over with Him? And say, 'Lord, here am I! How can, or may, or will I be of greater service to *you*, to my fellowman?' And leave it with Him! If you are sincere, if you are in earnest, if you will use your talents, let *Him* direct your way!" (622-6)

In 2156-1 Cayce said: "*All* who approach this channel [Cayce] may become assured in their lives and their experiences that God speaks to those who seek His face, who seek His ways." In this same exposition, Cayce explained that God is always ready to dialogue, but we shut off the dialogue: "Those who approach with the thoughts or with any phases of man's experience that cause distrust, envy, malice or the like, will shut and are shutting themselves, turning their faces away from a manifestation that would awaken that consciousness within their own hearts and souls that God, through His promise, is mindful of man."

How can we turn this around? How can we open the lines of communication again? Cayce guides us to "be oft in prayer, oft in seeking the manner, the way; that there may be brought into the experiences of this soul, this mind, a knowledge and an awareness of Christ as manifested in the life of Jesus—who so loved man as to give Himself as that sacrifice." But he goes on to explain that our mission is not sacrifice but love: "And now, here, it is not sacrifice that is required, but love—*love* made manifest; not materially, not in those things that corrupt or that make men afraid, but in the light of *God's* love—in conversation, in activities, in the dealing of one with another in the presence and in the consciousness of the entity." (2156-1) This touches on the teaching that God is love, and the more we manifest love in our thoughts, words, and actions, the closer we draw to God's conscious presence with us.

To Cayce, being close to God does not mean being a hermit or nun, but an active part of a family, a work place, a community: "Not that the entity is to be shut away from the world—but remember, as His prayer was, *keep* those about the entity from presumptuous sin, from that of hate, malice, jealousy; for these only make separations that will bring confusion into the experiences of this soul." (2156-1) Cayce identified hate, malice, jealousy, contention, backbiting, love of self, love of praise as "the spirit of the Antichrist," and he warned that there is a law against these: the law of karma. Karma is an actual force at work in people's lives. One cannot avoid the backlash of such negative energy in one's heart, mind, attitudes, and actions. But love, patience, understanding, kindness, and forgiveness are the spirit of the Christ light, and against these, Cayce said, there is no law, no limitation.

Cayce explained that acting like something *is*, while it actually is only a hope or an aspiration, builds a magnetic dynamic around which the reality may be realized. Therefore, living with a loving spirit towards others because one believes that God is love and one wants to know God more directly actually has the ultimate effect of attracting God and developing that closer relationship. Therefore, as strange as it may seem, begin acting like you and God have a dialogue and that you are close friends—let your thoughts, words, and actions reflect that closeness—

and before long, you'll consciously feel the friendship becoming increasingly real.

Overcoming Resistance and Limitations

Often life seems to block us from reaching and including God in our decisions and activities. Here's one person (911) who asked a question that all of us would like the answer to.

Q: How can I desire to be well, to accomplish things, and also fight family opposition and frustrations?

A: Only by the sheer will is there the desire to make beautiful the spirit of truth and life that gives animation to any desire of the body, the mind or the eye; and these conditions may *only* be met *by* that which has so oft been given: *Not in self,* but in the *inner* self—*the God that speaks within,* and in *giving* that, in thought, in act, in desire, for the welfare of others—*not of self!*—become *selfless!* Then there will grow that which makes the body, the mind, *strong*—able to meet every obstacle in the physical conditions, in the social surroundings, in the family circles, with a smile; knowing that "If my life is one with Him the rest matters *not,"* and *mean* it! and *do* it! and *be* it!   911-7

What a great answer.

Mrs. 911 pressed Cayce further with these following questions, and note that Cayce kept directing her toward selflessness and becoming a companion to the source of Life for all life.

Q: What is life for and what is expected of me?

A: Use that you have to the glorifying *not* of self but of the Spirit that gives Life itself, that you may *be* a companion with that source of Life that impels every thought, every desire, when not of a selfish nature. Using that you have for the satisfying of self's desires, self's own troubles, self's own conditions that arise, is being so self-centered as to destroy the good that may come to self.   911-7

Then 911 asked for the universal truth, and Cayce gave it to her and through her to us.

> Q: Please give me some universal truths that will best meet and help my consciousness and aid me in the material life.
> A: Study in body, mind, and soul to show yourself approved unto God, that gives eternal life; becoming less and less aware of the needs or *desires* that gratify the *carnal* forces in the body, and show that you have—by your prayer, your meditation—reached into the inner self sufficient to make self less and less *needful of* the material things; for what is life, that you gain power, position, wealth, and satisfy the longings of the flesh? Are you but to lose your own soul by so doing? It is in your keeping! He stands ready to help, if you will but *let* Him help! But if self bars the door to your consciousness, then indeed sad becomes the end!   911-7

Wow! How clear, straightforward, and specific is Cayce's wonderful answer. Notice also that Cayce indicated that God's way to us is through the door of our consciousness. It is as Ezekiel told us, "a still, small voice within." We *learn* how to commune with God in a give–and–take manner that allows for our expressions and God's insights.

Angelic Help

In addition to the inner voice, the inner dialogue, many of us today wonder about the role of angels in our spiritual communication and guidance, and here's an excellent Q and A in the Cayce work for us.

> Q: Is it through the guardian angel that God speaks to the individual?
> A: Ever through that influence or force as He has given, "You abide in me and I in you, as the Father abides in me, so may we make our abode with you." Then as the guardian influence or angel is ever before the face of the Father, through same may that influence ever speak—but only by the command of or attunement to that which is your ideal. What then is your ideal? In *whom* have you believed, as

well as in what have you believed? Is that in which you have believed able to keep ever before you that you commit unto Him?
Yes, through your angel, through your *self* that *is* the angel, does the
self speak with your Ideal!"   1646-1

Amazing! A part of each of us is an angel that is ever before the face
of our Father! What could possibly keep us from seeking direct contact
with our Papa and Mama now?

Prayer and Meditation

As most of us already know, Cayce's most common method for communing with God was through prayer and meditation. He defined
prayer as "talking to God" and meditation as "listening to God." He suggested that we use prayer to raise our consciousness into God's presence and then become quiet and receptive, feeling God's comfort and
guidance—as simple as that. So often we want God to make big ges-
tures, dramatic entrances, and booming commands, but God is gentle,
subtle, and so close to our consciousness that we can hardly tell His/
Her mind from our own. It requires that we become sensitive to subtle
feelings that come from deep within us while in God's presence. And if
these are unclear, then be patient, wait on the Lord to commune further,
ever believing that God will not leave us comfortless but will come to
us and commune with us. Practice, practice, practice prayer and meditation; results will come.

Dreams

In the book of Job (33:14-18), one of Job's friends, Elihu, makes a
statement that Cayce often made too: "For God speaks once, yes even
twice—though man doesn't regard it—in a dream, in a vision of the
night, when deep sleep falls upon men, in slumberings upon the bed.
Then He opens the ears of men, and seals their instruction, that He may
withdraw man from his [self-centered] purpose, and remove pride from
man. He keeps his soul back from the pit and his life from perishing by
the sword." Clearly, Elihu is telling Job, and us through Job, that God

uses dreams, night visions, to speak to us, to instruct us, and to protect us.

This makes great sense: since God is infinite and we are finite, the sleep state is perhaps one of the best conditions for us to be in when the Almighty, the Omnipotent, comes to us. If only we can make the transition to wakefulness the next morning with some memory of the conversation! That's an important part of this communication method, remembering what was said! We might add *understanding* what we remember. Understanding dreams is as important as remembering. The language of our subconscious seems so strange to our outer consciousness that it's like hearing an important message in a foreign language. Yet we can learn to understand subconscious imagery, symbolism, and its *implicit* messages—just as we can learn a foreign language. Cayce encourages all of us to do so.

But there's another tip on understanding dream messages—it comes from a great biblical dreamer, Joseph, one of the twelve sons of Jacob. Joseph teaches us to get the interpretation while still in the dreamy, sleep state, to "feel" the meaning of the dream before we completely awaken. This will give us a much better interpretation than trying to intellectually figure it out later with only our outer mind—a part of our mind that did not dream the dream. It is better to let our subconscious convey the meaning along with the message.

In reading 900-328 Cayce explained to Morton Blumenthal, who received more dream interpretations from Cayce than anyone else, that "in the dreams there comes more and more the better understanding of those conditions that are being presented through the various forms of the dissemination of knowledge in this material plane. And the body physically, mentally, may better understand the laws as apply in love apply in business, for force is as *one* force, and the ways of the Creative Energy are—and may be made—the ways of him who seeks to make self one with Him."

The Word

In closing, Mr. 877 asked Cayce a key question, and Cayce's answer gives us a faith statement that we need to hold on to while seeking direct conversation with God. But first, in order to fully grasp the questioner's intent, let me remind us that when Moses asked God to give him God's name in order that the people might know who was guiding them, God answered: "I Am that I Am." And Cayce explained that the little "I am" is a part of the great "I Am." Now here's the question and the answer we may hold as a faith statement:

> Q: Is it not true that the *The Word* mentioned in the first chapter of John's Gospel is the key to life? And is it not true that when man speaks the word "I Am" he directly links himself with God, the Absolute Power . . . [creating] the conditions of his own life, including his ability, his health, his environment, his conditions, and everything else in his personal universe?
>
> A: True! For, as He has given, "He that would know God must believe the understanding [comes] to everyone that diligently seeks Him."
>
> 877-2

How wonderfully exciting it is to know that even today, God speaks to those who seek His/Her companionship.

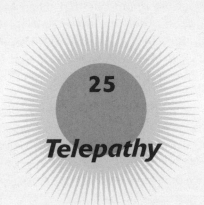

25

Telepathy

A.R.E. has published a new series of books by Edgar Cayce. Yes, I said *by Edgar Cayce!* The books are Cayce's readings on select topics: *Reincarnation and Karma, Soul and Spirit,* and *The Psychic Sense.* As the editor on this series. I came across a fascinating reading on telepathy in doing the research for the psychic sense book. I thought we could all benefit by studying this reading and applying telepathy in our lives.

Reading 792-2 began with Gertrude Cayce giving this suggestion to Edgar: "You will have before you the group of individuals who have been attempting elementary experiments in telepathy and card guessing on Thursday evenings in connection with the general work of the Association for Research and Enlightenment, Inc. Members of this group are present here. We desire to make our experiments of practical value, if possible, to each member of the group in relation to the individual mental and spiritual development and also make whatever contribution our development permits to the general knowledge of the laws of telepathy and simple clairvoyance. You will advise us regarding the right or proper procedure to obtain the best possible results."

After a moment or two, the "sleeping" Cayce responded: "Yes, we have the questions, we have the individuals, and those conditions that make same applicable in the experiences of those who have joined in the experiments thus far."

In the study of the phenomena of this nature, there should be first the questions and answers—or the analysis as to purpose—not only in the minds of those who would lend themselves in such an experience but in the minds of those who would preserve or present such experiments as a part of the research work of such an organization as the Association for Research and Enlightenment. As in this manner:

What is expected? What is the *source* of the information as may be had in such experiments, that goes beyond that called or termed the ordinary mind guessing? Or what is the basis of telepathic or clairvoyant communication? Or what are these in their elemental activity, or in all activity?

Now that Cayce has identified the key questions, he begins to give his perspective into workings of telepathy.

To be sure, the experience is a portion of the Mind; but Mind, as we have given, is both material *and* spiritual.

Now: From what order, or from what basis then, is such information sought by those who join in such experiments? It is the basis of all relationship of the individual entity to the cosmic or the universal forces. Or, to make it simple—yet most complex: "Know—the Lord thy God is *one! Know* the Lord thy God is *one!*"

Then the communications or the abilities for the activity of the Mind of an entity in such an experiment are *not* because of, or from, an association of entities. It is not then to be presumed, supposed, or proposed, to be a calling upon, a depending upon, a seeking for, that which is without—or that outside of self; but rather the attuning of self to the divine within, which is (the divine) a universal or *the* universal consciousness.

In these paragraphs, Cayce states that telepathy is an experience of a *portion* of the Mind—not the material mind but the spiritual one. He then explains that it is not a spiritual portion that is outside of oneself, as if passing through the air or from one mind to another. Rather, it is the unseen reality of a oneness that exists, and that oneness is accessed

from within us, not outside of us. The oneness is the cosmic, or universal, forces of the divine, within which we have our being. Our telepathic
development does not come from our relationship with the minds of
others but our relationship with the universal mind within which all
minds exist. He instructs us to "attune" ourselves to the divine *within* if
we would develop our telepathy.

Let's continue with the reading.

> [There will be found] those that are patterns or examples in Holy
> Writ; namely, an excellent one Saul, the first king. Here we find an
> example of an individual seeking from the man of God, or the
> prophet, information to be given clairvoyantly, telepathically (if you
> choose to use such terms); and we find the incident used as an
> illustration that may be well kept to the forefront in the Minds of
> those who would prompt or check or record such experiments.

Cayce is referring to passages in 1 Samuel, chapters 9 through 11, in
which Saul is watching over his father's animals when he decides to
visit the prophet Samuel to see what is envisioned for him. Samuel
explains that even before Saul arrived, God had "revealed" to him that
Saul would become ruler over many people. Upon receiving this prophecy, Saul wonders how he, from so small a tribe and the least among his
small tribe, could ever become a ruler over many. Ultimately, the "Spirit
of God" fills Saul's heart and mind, and his actions reflect the presence
of God's Spirit so that the people seek his leadership.

Now Cayce turns his attention to making telepathy practical.

> As to making practical application; it is what you do with the abili-
> ties that are developed by this attunement in coordinating, coop-
> erating one with another in such experiments. There are those in
> the group who have experimented that are gifted; gifted meaning
> then *innately* developed by the use of those faculties of the Mind
> to attune themselves to the Infinite.

This is an important point. *Gifted* means "innately developed" by the
use of telepathic faculties of the Mind attuned to the Infinite. Souls who

naturally have such abilities have developed them through previous use in prebirth experiences of their souls.

Now Cayce explains that there are others in the group who have not directly attuned themselves to the Mind of the Infinite but have been prompted to follow the guidance. Saul was not a direct seer as Samuel was, but he was prompted by Samuel to realize his potential. Here's that paragraph.

> Also there are those who have attuned themselves to a consciousness *not* wholly within themselves, but *prompted* by those who would become prompters—as in *any* attunement that is *ever* attempted in material consciousness, it is subject to same.

Now Cayce tells us that if we begin to feel drained by our practice of attunement for telepathy, then we are doing it wrong; we are creating static rather than a clear, natural channel. He explains that the universal consciousness is *constructive*, not destructive in any manner.

> When such an experiment, such a trial, draws or tires, or makes the mind foggy or dull or become as a drain upon the physical energies, know you are attuning wrong—and static has entered, from *some* source! For the universal consciousness *is* constructive, not destructive in *any* manner—but ever constructive in its activity with the elements that make up an entity's experience in the physical consciousness.

At this point, Cayce is ready for the group's questions.

> (Q) Please suggest the type of experiments which may be conducted most successfully by this group.
> (A) Well, you would have to take each as an individual—to say as to which may be the most successful! For there are grades, there are variations. These are in the group, as has been indicated, curiosity, wisdom, folly, *and* those things that make for real spiritual development. They each then require first—*first*—self-analysis! *What* prompts the individual to seek, engage, or desire to join in

such experiments? As to how far, as to what—there is no end! Is there any end to infinity? For this is the attunement, then—to Infinity!

Each will find a variation according to the application and the abilities of each to become less and less controlled by personality, and the more and more able to shut away the material consciousness—or the mind portion that is of the material, propagated or implied by what is termed the five senses. The more and more each is impelled by that which is intuitive, or the relying upon the soul force within, the greater, the farther, the deeper, the broader, the more constructive may be the result.

More and more, then, turn to those experiments that are not only helpful but that give hope to others, that make for the activity of the fruits of the Spirit.

Make haste slowly. Wait on the *Lord*; not making for a show, an activity of any kind that would be self-glorification, self-exaltation, but rather that which is helpful, hopeful for others.

Cayce has listed his key steps for success:

1. First—self-analysis! We need to know what is motivating us to become telepathic.

2. Less and less of our personality and more and more of our soul forces.

3. The results should not only be helpful but give *hope* to others.

4. Wait on the Lord, not making a personal show.

Notice also that the type of experiments that would help members develop would vary by each member's present need. Thus, the questions move from general to specific for each member. In reading these answers, we may find pertinence to our individual condition and needs as we develop telepathy.

(Q) [1406]
(A) This entity's experience and experiments will only be altered or hindered by self, and it may go as far into the field as is desired—so long as it keeps God and Christ *as* the ideal. Whenever there is the entering of other entities, or consciousnesses, or personalities—

be mindful of the ensample as is shown. Study that life, in association with such. Lose self more and more in the Christ Consciousness, if you would gain in those activities as may be thine, as may be seen by the soul development of this entity.

To each there is given the influence or spirit of direction. To some there is given the interpretation of tongues, or the interpretation of words or signs or symbols. This is what is meant by interpreters of tongues in the Holy Writ. To some is given healing; to some is given exhortation; to some is given ministration; to some is given one thing, some another.

Or, the *attunement* is the clarifier, or that which makes for clearer accord with that phase of the phenomena called clairvoyance, telepathy, or any psychic force of an entity.

In this particular body, we will find *any* of these—but the *most* will be given in healing, by the laying on of hands.

(Q) [1431]

(A) In exhortation; or attunements by discernment of activity—the application of individual self to such attunements.

Keep self towards not a *selfish* development, not a curious development, not for a famous development, but towards an *humbleness* of heart, an *humbleness* of purpose. For if you would know the truth, you must humble yourself; and then—as the experiments in the ability of attunements come—we may find self given more and more in exhortation; not exaltation, but exhortation.

(Q) [303]

(A) Here we find more and more that of a fearfulness, a hindrance by the holding to a physical consciousness. If there is the loss of self then to any extent, the physical consciousness, the deeper or better self may be given especially to bringing knowledge, understanding to others. For these are gained in self by giving out that you have. This is the secret of the whole process. You do not have until you give. You don't give to have, but you have because you give!

(Q) [562]

(A) Hold fast to the self within.

These all present different problems within their inner self for development, for hindrances, and for possibilities. To be sure, all of these suggestions are given from the constructive angle, with the hopes that none will—as Saul—partake of same for self's own indulgence, or self's own glory. [Here Cayce is referring to Saul's ultimate distraction by the trappings of wealth and power, and to his jealousy of David's rise to being God's chosen one.] But let the light, the *Love Divine*, be the guide; and we may find that those messages as for direction, as for help, may be thine.

(Q) [573]
(A) Again the warning not to look back, nor look to the *emotions* that arise from the sensitiveness of the sensory forces of the body; but rather to that which arises from the spiritual concept of an ideal. Thus we will find that visions of helpful warnings, of helpful admonitions, of helpful conditions for experiences that arise in the lives of others, may be thy part.
(Q) [1226]
(A) There is the tendency for worldly wisdom to confound the spiritual concept. Hence most of the common experiences become guesses, or the attempt to vision by mental-material visioning.

How many of us struggle with this challenge. Fortunately, Cayce gives 1226 some advice that we all can use:

Turn loose of self, then may the entity indeed be a teacher, a minister, to those who are weak, to those who are self-wise. But hold fast to Christ *in God*; and ye in Him! For as He has given, "As ye abide in me," so may there be brought to *your* remembrance that necessary for thy soul development, from the foundations of the earth. For if the Lord is One, and ye are one with Him, then it is as the current runs; or thy oneness with Him, as to the extent of thy ability to guide, direct, or to encourage those who are weak or lost in confusion of the times. Then with same, as in directing, will be healing.

(Q) [341]
(A) Keep hold on Him ever as thou hast seen and heard. "Is not this Him of whom the prophets spoke?" Thus ye will find that not the worldly wise, not the material or the physical consciousness, but the awareness of divine love will enable thee to help, direct, and hold in check, those tendencies for material expression from disincarnate entities.

Here Cayce warns Mr. 341 of his vulnerability to discarnates, a problem for many psychics who do not surround themselves with the protection found in the love for God-consciousness and the thought of Christ Consciousness.

Developing telepathy is a natural stage in our ongoing soul growth. We each should apply ourselves toward this development, working closely with God as our tutor, guide, and coach in this effort. All good gifts come from regular communion with our Creator. Cayce's tips give us a good start.

26

Diet for Higher Consciousness

*T*he Cayce discourses approach soul growth with a balanced physical, mental, and spiritual plan. We've read about the need to practice the fruits of the spirit and the importance of a good mental attitude that "replaces animosities, hates, and fears with faith, hope, longsuffering, patience and with the purposes not merely of self, but of self applying the principles of the Christ Consciousness." But according to Cayce's vision of the whole journey, *food* can help us spiritually and mentally. Indeed, the food we feed our bodies affects our minds and souls. There-fore, let's take a little time to consider some diet and exercise ideas given by Cayce to people seeking higher consciousness.

Before we get into this, we must remember that these readings were given to and affected by *individual* seekers and therefore may not be for all of us. Also, no plan is going to suit everyone. In one reading, Cayce told a seeker of Christ Consciousness that as he grew closer to this wis-dom, he would know from within himself what was best for his body. Let's explore Cayce's general diet and exercise plan for soul growth.

Breakfast

Since it breaks the night fast, the first meal of the day is especially important. I know some of us cannot eat in the morning; others are starving and like to have a big breakfast. Allowing for these personal differences, here's a typical Cayce breakfast pattern.

Alternate the following meals. On one day have a meal with citrus juice, the yolk of a coddled egg, wheat or rye toast, and coffee or tea. If you've grown accustomed to bacon, have a small amount, but cooked crisp. Special instructions were given not to burn it, but make it brown and crisp, with none of the grease in it, well drained. He recommended that we mix certain citrus juices to drink, adding lemon or lime to our orange juice or grapefruit juice (though in one reading, he did say that grapefruit doesn't need to be mixed with lemon or lime, and orange can be mixed with either; in twenty-one other readings he specifically recommended lime with the grapefruit juice and lemon with the orange juice). A coddled egg is a soft-boiled egg (cooked in the shell until the water begins to boil). The yolk is alkaline-producing, according to Cayce, while the white of an egg is acid-producing. The goal is to be slightly alkaline. Citrus juices are also alkaline-producing once in the body, even though they are citric acids. Cayce often said that the breakfast bread should always be brown, not white, and on a few occasions recommended that it always be toasted.

On another day, do not have citrus juices and eggs, but have grains, cereals. He preferred that we have the cooked varieties and that we alternate between whole grain wheat and oats (in most cases, steel-cut and well-cooked). These can be found in health food stores and some grocery stores. He did allow dry cereals but recommended the puffed varieties because they have the whole grain. Hot cereals are to be eaten with butter and salt, but milk can be an alternative; and if sweetening is needed, he suggested honey over sugar, though occasionally allowing for small amounts of sugar (preferably beet sugar or brown sugar, but not cane sugar). In several readings, he instructed seekers not to combine fruits with cereals, explaining that this mixture defeats the purpose of ingesting grains and properly assimilating their nutrients. Save the fruits for the egg breakfast, he suggested.

Lunch

In all cases, he recommended that raw vegetables be a part of the noonday meal, that they be as fresh as possible, and of a variety, so as not to bore the body. In the cases where physical problems were present, he almost always said to avoid vinegar and use oil, often olive oil, on the salad. For healthy people, he sometimes recommended red wine vinegar with oil, though he also recommended mayonnaise dressing on a salad. He always recommended vegetables grown above ground over those grown below; specifically, three above ground for every one grown underground. Also recommended was an occasional raw–fruit lunch with nuts, but not too many apples (he usually said to eat only cooked apples, but if raw, they were not to be eaten in combination with other foods). In several readings, he recommended lunchtime for soups (usually vegetable), broths, and the like, but usually for those who had physical problems. Meats could be eaten at lunch but never raw, rare, or fried, and no pork. Cayce suggested that we limit our meat eating to fish, fowl, and lamb, reducing the amount of red meat and eliminating pork (with the exception of his crisp bacon suggestion for breakfast). He often recommended a rest after lunch. He quoted the old saying, "After breakfast work awhile, after lunch rest awhile, after dinner walk a mile."

Dinner

For this meal he often suggested cooked vegetables and meats (within the restrictions just mentioned in the lunch plan). Vegetables cooked in, or eaten with, vinegar (a good old southern method) was discouraged. Again, he wanted a 3–to–1 ratio of vegetables that grow above ground to those that grow underground. He also discouraged consuming too many starchy vegetables (corn, dried beans, lima beans, peas, potatoes, sweet potatoes, and winter squash), preferring non–starchy vegetables (asparagus, broccoli, green beans, spinach, mushrooms, cabbage, cauli–flower, Brussels sprouts, eggplant, celery, and most leafy vegetables). Walking a mile following dinner was recommended for everyone. This may have been his way of enhancing metabolism in preparation for hours of slumber, in which the body is mostly inactive.

Other elements of the Cayce diet include gelatin, which he said was needed by the body in order to properly store nutrients gained from foods—"Not Jello, nor Royal but gelatin itself." Plain Knox Gelatin, available in grocery stores, is what he actually recommended, and then juices or vegetables can be added to it. He was most likely trying to avoid all the added sugar present in other dry gelatin mixes. In a few readings, he recommended stirring a half teaspoon of gelatin into cold water and drinking it (he specifically said not hot water). Here's a key reading on gelatin:

> Q: Please explain the vitamin content of gelatin. There is no reference to vitamin content on the package.
> A: It isn't the vitamin content but its ability to work with the activities of the glands, causing the glands to take from the absorbed or digested vitamins. See, there may be mixed with any chemical that which makes the rest of the system susceptible or able to call from the system that needed. It becomes then, "sensitive" to conditions. Without it there is not that sensitivity.   849-75

Another fascinating food combination in the readings is red wine and black bread (or dark bread). This certainly harkens back to Abraham and the high priest Melchizedek celebrating Abraham's love for others, so much love that he risked his own life to help another. Melchizedek broke bread and poured wine to celebrate this occasion. Later, Jesus announced that breaking bread and drinking wine would always be signs of a heavenly truth. In Jesus' case, the bread represented the body, and the wine the blood, each sacrificed for the sake of the mind and spirit. This would be a covenant, a sign of commitment and togetherness on the spiritual path. Cayce recommended that in the late afternoon, around an hour or two before dinner, we take a little red wine and dark bread. This would strengthen the blood, which would in turn help the body. Of course, there will be situations and circumstances in which this activity is inappropriate. But give it a try when you have an occasion to do so—not too much wine or you'll want to take a nap!

Exercise and Therapies

Of the many exercises and therapies recommended in the Cayce readings, walking and massage are among the most common and most beneficial to everyone. Cayce often suggested an Epsom salts bath or whirlpool bath before having a massage. The frequency depends upon the physical condition. The greater the physical problem(s), the greater the frequency. If the body is in pretty good shape, a regular schedule as benefits the body is recommended. Massage keeps the body's systems flowing and vital, from the lymph to the largest single organ in the body (and one we often forget to care for), the skin. By a process called reflex, surface rubbing of the body can help deeper internal circulation, organs, and nerve plexuses. Try to find a massage therapist that knows the Cayce–Reilly method of massage. But most of all, try to find a therapist that fits with your vibrations.

The level of our physical activity plays an important role in our diet and exercise. Cayce warned that a person who spends most of the day sitting at a desk cannot eat like a lumberjack. Those of us who have physically active lives and jobs will naturally need to eat differently than those who have sedentary lives.

Q: Spiritual foods?
A: These are needed by the body just as the body physical needs fuel in the diet. The body mental and spiritual needs spiritual food: prayer, meditation, thinking upon spiritual things. For thy body is indeed the temple of the living God.   4008-1

In the material plane it is necessary that material food values be taken for sustaining not only the physical forces but the spiritual elements as well; to keep them in contact or as parallel one to another in their activity.   516-4

The body is the temple. Keeping it in good condition is key to attaining Christ Consciousness, God–consciousness, and then channeling that light and love into everyone's life in this world. Healthy for a godly purpose, that's the best way.

During one of his most inspired readings, Cayce said that we could know "heaven on earth or in the earth, or in flesh." It is the "destiny of those that are willing, who have had their minds, their bodies, their souls cleansed in the blood of the Lamb. How? By being as He, a living example of that He, the Christ, professed to be." (262–77) "Flesh and blood has not revealed this to you, but my Father which is in heaven. Heaven? Where? Within the hearts, the minds; the place where Truth is made manifest!" (262–87)

From Cayce's trance perspective, the greatest evil in the earth and in the hearts and minds of individuals is contention, faultfinding, lovers of self, and lovers of praise, because these forces separate (281–16). The greatest good in the world is love, patience, kindness, forgiveness, and understanding, because these forces unite. "These are times when every effort should be made to preserve the universality of love." (877–29) He instructed one person to "study the truths about oneness, whether Jewish, Gentile, Greek, or heathen!" (136–12) Among religions, Cayce said that wherever the principle of one God and one people is taught, there is truth. And that in many of the world's great religions, the principle of oneness is there, but men have "turned this aside to meet their own immediate needs, as a moralist or the head of any independent power, but 'Know the Lord thy God is One!' whether this is directing one of the Confucius thought, Brahman thought, Buddha thought, Mohammedan thought . . . there is *only* one. The whole law and gospel of every age has said, 'There is *one* God!'" (364–9)

Again, the body is the temple and must be attended to physically, mentally, emotionally, and spiritually.

Spirit Body in the Womb of Consciousness

Section Five

STAYING ON TRACK

27

Keep On Keeping On

So many of us become weary from life's challenges (which often crush our hopes and dreams) and life's daily demands (which often are boring and mundane). When life becomes predominately physical, our physical self gets fatigued. Fatigue leads to weariness, and that leads to the blues. Then the weight of physical life brings us down. We slip further away from the rejuvenative, uplifting power of the Spirit. At times like this we must keep in mind that the Spirit does not tire or need sleep (the Great Spirit and our little spirits do not tire). Only our bodies and earthly portions grow weary. Therefore, being tired, depleted, and bored is a strong indication that we have slipped too deeply into material life and our material, physical nature. And yet, rather than get back into our spiritual practices, we stop or reduce them because we feel tired and need a break from it all. But the best medicine is to take time to lift ourselves into the Spirit. A little time in the Spirit can and will rejuvenate us, not just physically but mentally and emotionally as well. We will not only feel better, but our better self will come through and our perspective on life will improve.

When tired, seek time in the Spirit! Nothing can help us more. Here's how.

Take time to go sit quietly for at least a half hour. Get comfortable. Begin by gradually inhaling deeply, feeling your breath drawing up the energy from the lower parts of your body to the higher. Hold the breath at the top of your head and forehead. Now imagine the breath of God uniting with your breath. Just imagine it! Now gradually exhale and let this united breath bathe your body with its energy. Once completely exhaled, hold the breath there for a moment or two, feeling a deep quiet about your whole body. Now repeat the inhalation again, gradually and deeply. Feel strength as you draw the breath and the energy up your body to the top of your head and forehead. Hold it, and imagine the breath of God uniting with yours. Now once again gradually exhale, bathing your body in this united energy.

There is absolutely nothing but your own self that can keep God's breath from uniting with yours. Nothing! God is all-loving, all-merciful, all-present, and all-potent. Don't doubt. Don't wonder. Just do it! Just allow it! Only you can keep God from you. Let all your thoughts go. Allow God to join with your breath and rejuvenate you. Whatever issues you may have can be worked out later, when you are rejuvenated.

Once you have done enough of these breaths to feel some uplifting of your energy, let the breath go back on automatic. Now Edgar Cayce's readings instruct us to imagine (yes, use your "imaginative forces" is what he said) removing our "earthly portions and personality" from our body. Just "see, feel, know" that they are moving out and suspending in front of your body. Play with this; use that part of your mind that was your child mind. Imagine everything that is your earthly self and earthly life moving out of the way and suspending temporarily in front of you. The more you practice this, the better you'll get at doing it.

Now Cayce instructs us to "subjugate" control of our body and mind to our soul and subconscious. Allow the deeper subconscious mind and soul-self to take control of the system, to rise to a more present state of being. How? Imagine it. Use your child-mind to imagine your subconscious and soul taking control and becoming more present.

You know your soul. You are your soul. This is that part of you that dreams in sleep and survives physical death. And its mind, the subconscious, is that mind that manages all the autonomic nervous functions of your body, functions you have no idea how to manage consciously (breathing, heart rate, digestion, sensory processing, and so on). Subjugate control to your soul and subconscious.

Now Cayce instructs us to use a powerful suggestion to lift ourselves into the universal mind and spirit of God. The subconscious is always amenable to suggestion. Give it a repetitive suggestion to rise into the universal mind and spirit of God. You can use any phrase that conveys this. I use: "Arise my soul, and enter into the Universal Consciousness and the Infinite Spirit of God." I imagine the Universal Consciousness, not so much by visualizing it, but by feeling it. I feel that infinite, vast, all-encompassing mind of God, in which all of life has its being. This expands me as I do it. I feel myself expanding out from my little point of finite mind into this infinite mind. It feels good, freeing. Then I feel the powerful yet gentle spirit of God. It feels like (and of course is) the source of all life. At the point that I get my first sense of God's mind and spirit, I say the Cayce phrase: "Not my will, but Thine." I then feel God's life force flow into me. Originally I imagined it, but now I truly feel it flow into me. As it flows in, I, like a surfer on a wave, allow it to lift me up into its Presence more fully and go with it. I attempt to abide in this Presence as long as possible, without moving or thinking. I'm just "in the Spirit," for as long as I can be. I try not to ask questions or request help or cry the blues. I don't even pray for anyone or anything. It's a time to just be still and allow God's will and life force to do Its thing the way It sees best.

However, once I have been imbued with the Spirit and feel that the session is drawing to a close, I then bring up issues and people that I'm concerned about, in hopes of getting some insight or guidance. Sometimes I get these, sometimes not. But my physical self and my physical life are always better for having spent time in the Spirit. Even if problems persist, my perspective and attitude are always better than if I hadn't taken the time to do this. My body also feels strengthened by the experience.

As the session is ending, I also direct the Spirit toward others through prayer.

Don't let life wear you out or down. Make time to get up into the ever-ready Spirit. The flesh is weak but the Spirit is always ready and willing to rejuvenate and enlighten. Seek time in the Spirit.

28

Turn to the Light

Sometimes the rhythms of life that bring happiness are clouded by uncertainty or confusion, resulting in anxiety and even fear. The reasons are many—they can be related to health or finances, relationships, loss of a sense of purpose, or worry for others. In the philosophy from Edgar Cayce's attunement to the Universal Consciousness, we find tips on how to deal with life's challenges, such as this one: "If you live in the light, the shadows fall behind. If your face is turned from the light, there can be nothing in the life—in the mental or material things—*but* shadow. *Turn to the Light!*" (257-123) Another way that he said this was, "Turn thy face to the light and the shadows fall behind." (987-4)

An old Swedish saying that well reflects Cayce's turn–to–the–light admonition is, *Worry often gives a small thing a big shadow.* A classic saying is, *Worrying never changed anything.* Cayce often asked us, "Why worry when you can pray?"

During those times of uncertainty or unexpected change, it helps to recall sayings that have been handed down through the ages from one generation of struggling humans to another, like this Confucian one: *Grandfather say, "It does not rain every day."* Of course, on a hard–rain day it feels like it will never let up again. But, as my mother used to say to me, "This too will pass."

Cayce encouraged us to use our will and make a decision, right or wrong. This is better than doing nothing. However, Cayce also admonished us to make the decision based on our ideals, not on our circumstances, as this old saying indicates: *Following the path of least resistance is what makes both men and rivers crooked.* We should set our goals before taking action, as this old German proverb suggests: *What good is running when you're on the wrong road.*

The role of our will is expressed in this old Chinese saying: *If you fall into a pit, you either die or get out.* Let's get out!

The Japanese have a great old saying: *We learn little from victory, much from defeat.* And Horace, of classical fame (65–8 BC), had two good tips for us in hard times: *What may not be altered is made lighter by patience,* and *When life's path is steep, keep your mind even.* And if we're feeling sorry for ourselves, an old Armenian saying asks us: *Where is there a tree not shaken by the wind?* Challenges are simply a part of living in this world. They build strong human character, as the wind builds strong trees.

An old African saying is a good one to keep in mind during trouble: *When there is no enemy within, the enemies outside cannot hurt you.* This is like Cayce's claim that the only limitation is self, "That which has passed is past. That continually 'dug up' will continue to be a sore spot. That which is gone, let it be gone. Turn your face to the light in Him." (1561–18) "Nothing prevents—only self. Keep self and the shadow away. Turn thy face to the light and the shadows fall behind." (987-4)

Ben Franklin had a volume of wise old sayings to help us. As for self's role in many of our problems, he asked, "Who is strong? He that can conquer his bad habits." When it came to being hurt by the words or actions of another, he wrote: "Write injuries in dust, benefits in marble." And when it came to financial problems, he had this clever little insight to share with us: "Who is rich? He that enjoys his portion."

If our challenge is another person's problems, then here is a good old saying passed down to us from Aesop, of Aesop's Fables (ca. 620–560 BC): "Give assistance not advice in a crisis." And a great one of unknown origin reminds us of our fellowship, *Friends are God's way of taking care of us.*

29

Life

*R*eading 5753-1 is one of Edgar Cayce's most interesting and helpful readings. Once he tuned himself to the higher forces, his wife, Gertrude, gave this suggestion, which guided the whole discourse: "You will give at this time a comprehensive discourse on reincarnation. If the soul returns to the earth through a succession of appearances, you will explain why this is necessary or desirable and will clarify through explanation the laws governing such returns. You will answer the questions which will be asked on this subject."

From his attunement to the Universal Consciousness, Cayce replied to the suggestion: "In giving even an approach to the subject sought here, it is well that there be given some things that may be accepted as standards from which conclusions or parallels may be drawn. [In this way] there may be gathered some understanding, some concrete examples, that may be applied in one's own individual experience."

The First Cause

Cayce wanted to establish a foundation from which we could develop our own conclusions and parallels. He explained that the reincarnation journey is not a journey of our outer self; rather, it is a journey of our inner soul self. He then asked us to consider this: What is our soul's "impetus" to live, to experience life? Why does the soul enter into these lives and relationships, with all of their ups and downs, their joys and sorrows? Cayce saw a single impetus. He called it the "First Cause," meaning the first cause for our existence. Cayce identified the first cause as this: "That the created would be the companion for the Creator." This is the reason behind our creation, and as a result, the created (our soul) is given opportunities to "show itself to be not only worthy of, but companionable to, the Creator."

The Soul's Motivation

Cayce then clarified that the soul, the offspring of the Creator, enters into every situation and relationship longing to develop abilities and qualities that "demonstrate, manifest, show forth, and reflect" its efforts towards realizing the first cause: to make itself companionable to its Creator.

In practical terms, the very next human being that walks up to us is an opportunity for us to relate in a manner reflective of our companionableness to our Creator or not. The circumstances of our life are opportunities to think and act with a *Creator-companionable* attitude or not. Good, in this model, is anything that leads *toward* greater companionship; evil leads *away* from it.

Of course, souls lose awareness of the first cause for their existence. They become distracted by self-indulgence and self-centeredness. Some have so lost contact with this purpose that they let life's circumstances determine the direction of their lives, or they let others make the important choices for them.

Paradoxically, we, God's created, are also cocreators with our Creator in such a way that we are the cause and the effect!—with free will and creative freedom with cause. What we do with free will and creativity builds our circumstances and consciousness! "Hence man, the crowning of all manifestations in a causation world, finds self as the cause *and* the product of that he, man, has been able to produce or demonstrate."

Knowing What Is Best

At this point in the discourse, Cayce presented the law of "like begets like." What a soul has done with its attributes in the past affects its circumstances and relationships today. Cayce observed that our very next use of free will determines our soul's next situation. Rather than weep or whine over yesterday's mistakes, it's better for us to get up and do good *today*, for *tomorrow* will be affected by such.

At this point, Cayce presented an important yet surprising principle: We, our souls, *already know* what we should be doing and what is right and wrong for us. This awareness comes into this life and body with us at birth and is with us throughout our incarnation. How do we know what is right or wrong? The readings describe how our deeper self is always correlating what is happening with what is known to be best for achieving the first cause. Cayce explained that we will "feel" in accord with thoughts and actions that lead toward companionship with our Creator. A "contrariness," however, warns of discord with the soul's reason for existence.

How does this appear in daily life? We have all said something, only later to feel bad about having said it. We have all done something, only later to feel disappointed with ourselves for having done it. These indicators bubble to the surface of our consciousness as our deeper self correlates and compares our words and actions with what would have been more in line with our soul's purpose for existence. We call this our *conscience*. If we learn to listen to it, it will guide us toward better situations and relationships.

Spiritual Food

Then, Cayce moved to a lesson about feeding ourselves, not physically but mentally. He began by stating his well-known axiom "mind is the builder" but then gave a little twist on it, remarking that what the mind is fed, it becomes. "When an entity fills its mind with those experiences that bespeak of the carnal forces, the mind becomes carnally directed. If one's mind is filled with those things that bespeak of the spirit, that one becomes spiritual-minded."

Cayce identified carnal forces as those that generate "envy, strife, contention, selfishness, greediness, avarice, hate, and the like." Spiritual food for the mind is generated by "kindness, brotherly love, good deeds, and patience," what the Bible calls the "fruits of the Spirit." Cayce remarked that hearts and minds fed on such feel "the Spirit of the Light."

Here the reading warns us to be careful of "experiences that satisfy or gratify self without thought of the effect upon its own relation to the first cause!"

God—Our Companion

Imagine the nature of the omnipotent, omnipresent One. Imagine how we would have to grow to become companionable to the Infinite One. Jesus told the woman at the well that God is a *Spirit* and seeks us to commune in spirit. The simple secret is that God is found in the *fruits* of the Spirit. It is a simple path in principle but often a hard one in daily application.

Cayce said that the soul is naturally immortal but finds reincarnation (physical life and death) to be a helpful way to try again, to grow a little more. As Cayce noted, we don't *go* to heaven; we *grow* to heaven. Reincarnation is a merciful way of allowing souls to have several opportunities to subdue selfishness and enhance cooperation with the Creator and the Creative Forces.

Cayce allowed that "a soul may will itself *never* to reincarnate, but [then] must burn and burn and burn—or suffer and suffer and suffer! For, the heaven and hell is built by the soul! The companionship to God is being one with Him; and the gift of God is being conscious of being one with Him." The alternative to burning and suffering is to find situations and relationships that allow the soul to work through its incompatible thoughts and actions toward compatible ones.

Here Cayce remarked, "A soul is as real as a physical entity, and is as subject to laws as is the physical body! Does fire burn the soul or the physical body? Yet, self may cast self into a fire element by doing that the soul knows to be wrong!" Therefore, the soul itself seeks out opportunities to resolve incompatibilities. Cayce taught that as we *forgive* others, we are *forgiven*; as we understand others, we are understood; and as we forget what others have said or done to us, what we have said or done is forgotten. *Like begets like* is the law that leads to resolution of all problems. Any soul can change its thoughts and actions and thereby change itself and its tomorrows.

Christ's Power to Help Us

At this point in the reading, Cayce moved on to an important yet touchy concept, especially given today's sensitivities toward religious extremism. Yet, when one reads the whole of Cayce's discourses, it becomes clear that he was more interested in the principles that are *universally* spiritual than those that are selectively promoting a single religion. Obviously, Cayce's readings are founded in Judeo–Christian concepts but with a mystical, universal view. From Cayce's perspective, Christ is a universal Spirit that guides and helps all souls. Cayce said that "the Christ Consciousness is a universal consciousness of the Father Spirit" (5749–4), again touching on the Creator and the created's destiny together as parent and offspring.

Cayce stated his next principle: "It is as was given by Him, 'I am the way. No man approaches the Father but by me.' But, does a soul crucify the flesh even as He, when it finds within itself that it must work out its own salvation in a material world, by entering and re–entering? Rather is the law of *forgiveness* made of effect in your experience, through Him that would stand in your stead; for He is the way, that light *ever ready to aid* when there is the call upon, and the trust of the soul in, that first cause!"

Cayce explained that we are not to crucify our bodies, but rather we are to crucify our selfish desires in order to allow the Creator's desires to take hold, helping us to become companionable. Cayce expounded on this thought, saying, "The consciousness in the soul" has to make itself "a companion with the Creator." We, individually, have to choose to seek companionship and to make ourselves companionable. No one can do it for us. We must use our free wills to *seek* it and *work* toward it.

Cayce added that we have some powerful help in reaching our first cause for existence: companionship with God. Cayce said that we may take hold of, call upon, and trust in the Creator's love for us. As Jesus explained in John 14:26–28: "The Counselor, the Holy Spirit, whom the Father will send in my name, he will teach you all things." In John 16:7, Jesus said: "It is expedient for you that I go away; for if I do not go, the Comforter will not come to you; but if I go, I will send him to you." By making himself completely companionable with the Father/Mother, Jesus was able to send us a powerful helper, the "Spirit of Truth." This Spirit is both a counselor and a comforter.

In our seeking to realize our soul's first cause for existence, the Spirit of Truth is a powerful resource. That is, if we invite it into our consciousness and, like cocreators, allow it to work with us in life's decisions. A true companion is one that *cooperates*—neither surrendering its free will nor rebelling against any aligning of its will with God's. It is a magic duet of Creator and created.

Spiritualization, Not Separation

Finally, our path is not a resurrection *away* from the physical, but a *spiritualizing* of the physical by getting beyond self-centered physicality, beyond thinking and acting alone. If we awaken to our conscience and the Spirit of Truth within us, we will realize how much unseen help and guidance is available to us. As a soul opens to its inner companionship with its Creator and the Creative Forces, our whole being becomes *companionable* to the Creator.

Cayce wanted us to try living, thinking, speaking, and acting in harmony with the first cause for our existence: becoming companionable to our Creator, who is also the Creator of other souls and everything in the Cosmos. Such a disposition will lead to a deep sense of fulfillment and ultimate happiness and contentment. Why? Because such a disposition is our primary reason for our existence. Cayce described our ideal disposition this way: "To know yourself to be yourself, yet one with the Whole." The "Whole" is the omnipotent, omnipresent Creator.

30

Purpose

*H*ere is a large except from reading 3976–29. I have done minor edit-
ing for clarity and focus on the main points. [Bracketed comments are
mine, not Cayce's.]

EC: When there came about the periods of man's evolution in the
earth, what was given as to why man must be separated into
tongues, into nations, into groups? "Lest they in their foolish wisdom defy God." What is intimated by this? That man, seeking his
own gratification of the lusts of the flesh, might even in the earth
defy God.

With what, then, has man been endowed by his Creator? All
that would be necessary for each individual soul-entity to be a
companion with God. And that is God's desire toward man. Thus
when man began to defy God in the earth and the confusion arose
which is represented in the Tower of Babel; nations were set up in
various portions of the land, and each group, one stronger than
another, set about to seek their gratifications.

It isn't that God chose to reserve or save anything that was good
from man, so long as man was, is, and will be one who uses that
living soul as a companion with God. That's God's purpose. That
should be man's purpose.

Remember, there are unchangeable laws. For God is law. Law is God. Love is law. Love is God. There are then in the hearts, the minds of man, various concepts of these laws and as to where and to what they are applicable. Then, just as in the days of old, the nature of the flesh, human flesh and human nature, has not changed. But the spirit maketh alive. The truth maketh one free. For God meant man to be free and thus gave man will, a will even to defy God. *God* has not willed that any soul should perish, but hath with every trial or temptation prepared a way of escape.

There have come through the various periods of man's unfoldment, teachers proclaiming "This is the way; Here is the manner in which ye may know," and yet in the Teacher of Teachers is found the way, He who even in himself fulfilled the law. For when God said, "Let there be light" there came Light into that which He had created, that was without form and was void and it became the Word, and the Word dwelt among us and we perceived it not. The Word today dwells among us and many of us perceive it not.

Those nations who have taken those vows that man shall be free should also take those vows: "He shall know the truth and the truth then shall make him free."

Then what is this that would be given thee today? Here is thy lesson: Hear ye all! Beware lest ye as an individual soul, a son, a daughter of God, fail in thy mission in the earth today; that those ye know, those ye contact shall know the truth of God, not by thy word, bombastic words, but in longsuffering, in patience, in harmony, that ye create in thine own lives, for it must begin with thee. God has shown thee the pattern, even one Jesus, who became the Christ that ye might have an advocate with the Father. The Father hath said "In the day ye eat or use the knowledge for thine own aggrandizement, ye shall die [symbolized by the apple in the Garden]." But he [the serpent] that had persuaded the souls to push into matter to gratify desire for self-expression, self-indulgence, self-satisfaction, said "Ye shall not surely die." As had been said, "A day is a thousand years, a thousand years as a day." [Here Cayce was giving us an indication of how time for the soul is so different than it is for man that there was some truth in the serpent's statement. There really is no death, but loss of direct contact with God would feel like death. Yet, in time, we would awaken to the truth again.]

What was the length of life then? Nearly a thousand years. What is your life today? May it not be just as He had given, just as He indicated to those peoples, just as He did to the lawgiver, just as He did to David—first from a thousand years to a hundred and twenty, then to eighty? Why? Why? The sin of man in his desire for self-gratification.

Look to the nations where the span of life has been extended from sixty to eight-four years. You will judge who is serving God. These are judgments. These are the signs to those who seek to know, who will study the heavens, who will analyze the elements, who will know the heart of man. They that seek to know the will of the Father for themselves answer "Lord, here am I, use me, send me where I am needed."

Just as have been those principles of your present conflict [WWII]. "Send help, for man's heritage of freedom will be taken away." By whom? He that hath said, "Surely ye will not die." There are those two principles, two conflicting forces in the earth today: the prince of this world, and that principle that says to every soul, "Fear not, I have overcome the world and the prince of the world hath nothing in me." Can ye say that? Ye must! That is thy hope; that "The prince of this world, satan, that old serpent, hath no part in any desire of my mind, my heart, my body, that I do not control in the direction it shall take." These are the things, these are the principles.

Then apply in thine own life *truth*. What is truth? It might have been answered, had an individual entity who stood at the crossways of the world waited for an answer. [Cayce is referring to Pontius Pilot, who asked Jesus, "What is Truth?" but then did not wait for an answer.] Yet that soul [Jesus] had purified itself and had given the new commandment that "ye love one another!"

What is it all about then? "Thou shalt love the Lord thy God with all thine heart, thine soul, thine mind, thine body, and thy neighbor as thyself." The rest of all the theories that may be concocted by

man are nothing, if these are just lived. Love thy neighbor as thyself
in thy associations day by day. Know, then, that as He had His cross,
so have you. May you take it with a smile. You can, if ye will let Him
bear it with thee. Do it.

In this wonderful reading we find the core truth to live by. We find
the source of our troubles and the end thereof. Self-seeking leads away
from God; loving and caring leads toward reunion with God. And since
God created us to be His/Her companions, anything that leads away
from companionship is death and failure to our mission, our purpose
for existing.

A subtle but important element of this mission is that others are not
separate beings from God, as much as they may appear to be. God
contains everything and everyone. God created them and desires companionship with them. Therefore, we not only have to love God but
also those we meet day by day. Others are part of the whole picture, the
whole plan. Perhaps this is why Jesus said that the second commandment is like the first. Loving others is loving God, because all souls are
part of God and God's plan.

I like the way Cayce ended the reading by simply saying, "Do it." Too
often we spend time thinking about it or planning it or intending to do
it. The instruction is to just do it, now, and day by day.

31

Remain Content

*T*here are so many helpful principles in the Edgar Cayce discourses. One of my favorites is "be *content*, but *never* satisfied!" (1723–1) Cayce explained that "it is not well that any soul or mind should be satisfied, for that indicates staleness, lack of growth. Be content!" Contentment, from Cayce's perspective, is using what one has at hand because it is sufficient to make growth in a step–by–step manner, which is the better way to grow. "Be content, ever working toward that oneness of mind, of body, of will, with the development, or with the universal or psychic forces. Do not war against life's conditions. Make of conditions the stepping–stones to the development necessary to meet the daily needs in physical, in mental, in financial." (137–7)

For example, rather than "war" with the challenges or limitations of our job, finances, relationships, physical health, or whatever it is we struggle with, let's set a course that will gradually lead us to a new condition, and let's proceed along that course with a patient, contented spirit and attitude. Also, we often believe that we don't have what is needed to get us out of our circumstances or to stop our bad habits, but we just need to use whatever we have at hand, taking one little step, in order to begin the journey to a new and improved condition.

Cayce explained that "contentment can only arise in anyone from the *ideals* of self being manifest, rather than hidden or questioned by self or another." (279-15) In other words, setting our ideals (physically, financially, mentally, emotionally, spiritually) and then *manifesting* those ideals in our daily efforts—not only physical efforts but emotional and attitudinal efforts, such as thinking more positively, reacting less defensively or angrily, and the like.

Of course, Cayce often lifted our thoughts to the spiritual level of activity, as in this statement and those that follow: "Content in that 'Have Thy way, Lord. Use me as a channel. Not my will but Thine be done!' That is content. Satisfied means gratified, and is the beginning of the falling away, for self is to be then glorified. He that is satisfied has ceased to grow." (262-24) Allowing God's will to guide us, to open the way before us, subdues our egocentric notions and impulses, making us alert to synchronistic opportunities that seem to come from out of nowhere.

"The entity's application to an ideal founded within self and self's own soul's development has brought that of a contentment that is found seldom in individual experiences. Not satisfied, no, for then the entity would begin to lose. But being content and being satisfied are different conditions in a soul's experience. One may be content that they may be guided by that of an ideal towards which the entity would make its soul or its peace one with that ideal. Satisfied in the labors given, or in the service rendered, is to become sterile and unfruitful in the activities. As has oft been given, in the doing does the understanding come." (1466-1)

"Be happy in well doing, content in that as is in hand, satisfied only in continuing in *striving* to do well." (1000-8)

TWO GOOD MEDITATION METHODS

32

Cayce's Complete Method

*I*n chapter 3 of the Gospel according to John, Nicodemus sought wisdom from Jesus. Jesus gives him insight into three mysteries. The first
has become quite well known: "Unless a man is born again, he cannot
see the kingdom of God. That which is born from the flesh is flesh, and
that which is born from the Spirit is spirit." Meditation helps us achieve
the second birth by birthing the Spirit within us. The second wisdom
piece is that "no one ascends to heaven but he or she who already
descended from heaven." We have all come down from heaven, though
we have lost memory of our former selves and our former oneness with
our Creator. At the Last Supper, Jesus tells Thomas, "You know where I
am going and you know the way." (John 14:4) Thomas, like most of us,
cannot understand how he could know the way to the Father, since he
is a man of only fifty years. Of course, Jesus was not speaking of our
outer, earthly self. Our deeper, soul–self descended from heaven and
knows the way to heaven, though it is now a dormant instinct that
must be reawakened—and meditation helps us do just that. The third
wisdom message relates directly to the fall of the serpent in the Garden
of Eden, those faraway times when our soul first descended from heaven
and human nature began. Jesus says to Nicodemus: "As Moses raised
the serpent in the desert, so must the Son of Man be raised up." If we
read Genesis carefully, we'll notice that not only did Adam and Eve fall

in the Garden of Eden, but the serpent fell also. Later, when Moses is out in the desert searching for his true identity and his connection to God, he comes across seven maidens attempting to water themselves and their flocks from a deep well, but other herdsmen keep pushing them away. Moses, one man, drives off all the other herdsmen and waters the seven virgins and their flocks. Then the maidens tell him that they are daughters of a high priest and take Moses to the tent of the high priest. Eventually Moses marries the eldest daughter. Later he meets God in a flaming bush. The first lesson God teaches Moses is how to raise the serpent off the desert floor and turn it into a power staff, a staff that will once again bud, and life and power will flow through it.

Nicodemus was educated in the Scriptures. He would have known this event of Moses' and the details surrounding it. He may even have known that the story relates not just to seven maidens but to the seven spiritual centers within Moses, and how the outer world's forces keep us from watering our spiritual centers. These seven centers are the "daughters" of our higher self, and to unite with the highest center (marry the eldest daughter) is to awaken the flame of the Spirit at the crown of our head (the tongue of flame atop the "bush" of our hair). God's voice will speak to us and guide us in raising the life force within our bodies and budding anew our dormant abilities.

Eventually, Moses is able to ascend the mountain and enter into the presence and the power of God, the Omnipotent.

The Sanskrit word *kundalini* means "coiled serpent." It is used to convey how the life force of the body is like a coiled serpent lying in the lower spiritual centers of our bodies, waiting to rise up like a cobra enchanted by the music of the charmer's flute. Not surprisingly, the ancient Kabalists and Gnostics used the Hebrew word *speirema* (meaning "serpent coil") to describe the lower center in the human body.

As we know, there are seven spiritual centers through which the life force moves along three pathways. One pathway is the central nervous system's cerebrospinal column, and the other two are intertwined double-helix pathways called *ida* and *pingala*, representing the sympathetic and parasympathetic twins of the autonomic nervous system.

The seven spiritual centers have a dual nature. They are chakras, "spinning wheels" of energy, and padmes, "lotuses" of illuminating fragrance, carrying the sense of heaven. Therefore, each center is both a physical energy wheel and a consciousness–expanding flower of illumination.

As Cayce relates, these seven spiritual centers are directly related to the seven endocrine glands within our bodies. The endocrine glands secrete hormones directly into our bloodstream, causing our bodies to change according to whatever message the hormones are carrying. If we are calling on the body to raise its vibrations and reverse the flow of energy and consciousness toward the heavens and away from the earth, then the hormone message changes accordingly, helping the whole of the body achieve this goal.

Because of the transformative powers involved in meditation, there are some warnings in the Edgar Cayce readings about meditating without proper preparation and self–examination.

Warnings

"But make haste *slowly*! Prepare the body. Prepare the mind, before ye attempt to loosen it in such measures or manners that it may be taken hold upon by those influences which constantly seek expressions of self rather than of a living, constructive influence of a *crucified* Savior. Then, crucify desire in self; that ye may be awakened to the real abilities of helpfulness that lie within thy grasp . . . Without preparation, desires of *every* nature may become so accentuated as to destroy . . . " (2475–1) Therefore, let's examine our purposes, searching our hearts for our true passion. Is it cooperation and coordination with God, or are we still longing to gratify some lingering desires of our own self–interests?

As mentioned in chapter 20, "Getting Guidance," the Taoist meditation teachers in the ancient texts of *The Secret of the Golden Flower* talk about the right method being like one wing of a bird, and the other wing being the right heart. The wise meditator must remember that the bird cannot fly with only one wing. We have to have the right method and the right heart—or the right motivating influence.

The Ideal

The right-heart concept leads us naturally to the Cayce readings' teaching that an ideal should be raised as we seek to awaken the life force. What is our ideal? To whom or what do we look for examples of better behavior, better choices, better uses for our energies, and better relating skills with others? What standard guides us in conceiving our better selves? Who is the author of our "Book of Life"? Is it the circumstances of life? Is it our self-interests?

These are important questions from the perspective of the Cayce readings, questions that should be considered before going on with the powerful kundalini forces aroused in this method of meditation. As the readings say, we can build a Frankenstein or a god using basically the same meditation method. It all depends on the ideal held as the practice progresses.

> *Find* that which is to *yourself* the more certain way to your consciousness of *purifying* body and mind, before ye attempt to enter into the meditation as to raise the image of that through which ye are seeking to know the will or the activity of the Creative Forces; for ye are *raising* in meditation actual *creation* taking place within the inner self!   281-13

The readings would advise anyone who feels unable to "set the carnal aside" and attune to a high ideal for the period of meditation not to meditate; and instead to pray. If the prayer then changes you and you feel that you can set the carnal forces aside, you may enter into meditation. Otherwise, stay away from it. Meditation gives power to whatever is in the consciousness and desires of the person. Make sure these are pure and of the highest ideal.

Jesus Christ

The Cayce readings present Jesus Christ as not only a high ideal but as a powerful force of protection for anyone seeking to loosen one's life force, to open the biospiritual seals, and enter into the presence of God.

Christ is presented as our advocate before the Godhead. To call on this protection and guidance is to call on the greatest resource available. However, the readings do not put the religion that formed around Jesus Christ above other religions. The readings are too universal for that. Seekers from any religious faith can use the power of Christ in their meditation practice and still remain loyal to their religion. Here's an example of this perspective, excerpted from reading 281-13:

> If there has been set the mark (mark meaning here the image that is raised by the individual in its imaginative and impulse force) such that it takes the form of the ideal the individual is holding as its standard to be raised to . . . then the individual (or the image) bears the mark of the Lamb, or the Christ, or the Holy One, or the Son, or any of the names we may have given to that which enables the individual to enter *through it* into the very presence of that which is the creative force from within itself; see? . . .
>
> Raising, then, in the inner self that image of the Christ, love of the God-consciousness, is making the body so cleansed as to be barred against all powers that would, in any manner hinder.

Notice that "Christ" is given as equivalent to the "love of God-consciousness." Seekers from any religion may have love of God-consciousness. Christ in this perspective is more universal than the religion that possesses that name. Notice also that "love of God-consciousness" cleanses us of self-interests that may hinder or harm us.

However, there is much more to this reading than ecumenism and protection. Cayce is giving us a great insight into just how a meditator may be transported from a good meditative stillness into the very presence of the Creative Force, God, with all the ramifications of such an experience. If, in our imaginative forces, we can conceive or form the ideal (the standard) to which we seek to be raised, then we (as the Revelation states) bear the mark, or the sign, of that power (whatever name we give it) that enables us to enter through it into the very presence of God within us, the Creative Force within us. Despite the power of some of the other techniques in this form of meditation, imagining the ideal is seminal to transformation. Reading 1458-1 points out our only limitation: "The entity is only limited to that it sets as its ideal." We are "gods in the making" if we can conceive ourselves to be such, in cooperation and coordination with the Great God.

The Kundalini and Eternal Life

As we have seen, the readings interweave Judaeo-Christian teachings found throughout the Old and New Testaments, but particularly in the book of Revelation, with concepts and practices from ancient Hinduism and Yoga. The fundamental concepts are these: The kundalini is metaphorically seen as the great serpent power fallen from its original place of honor. As Adam and Eve fell from grace in the Garden, so did the serpent. But, as Moses raised the serpent in the desert and Jesus raised it to life everlasting, so each of us must raise our serpent power to its rightful, original place of honor. Kundalini meditation is intended to do just that.

This kundalini, or life force, is within the human body, the temple. Normally it is used in ways that dissipate it, eventually leading to aging and death of the body. All people are allowed to use their life force as they choose (at least within the confines of their karma). Whether they dissipate it consciously or unconsciously makes no difference. When it's gone, it's gone. But it doesn't have to be this way. As the readings put it, "If there will be gained that consciousness, there need not be ever the necessity of a physical organism aging . . . Seeing this, feeling this, knowing this, ye will find that not only does the body become revivified, but by the creating in every atom of its being the knowledge of the activity of this Creative Force . . . spirit, mind, body [are] renewed." (1299-1)

The *élan vital* of the Western world and the *kundalini* of the Eastern world follow natural laws and can be made to flow in rejuvenative ways that enhance and extend the life. This is not only possible with kundalini meditation, but it is a valuable goal to pursue. Here's one reading's statement on this: "How is the way shown by the Master? What is the promise in Him? The last to be overcome is death. Death of what? The *soul* cannot die, for it is of God. The body may be revivified, rejuvenated. And it is to that end it may, the body, *transcend* the earth and its influence." (262–85) This meditation practice works directly with the forces of life.

Head-and-Neck Exercise

Cayce designed a specific head–and–neck exercise to use in preparation for meditation. It will loosen up the kundalini pathway within our bodies and get the fluids and electrical energies flowing.

Tilt the head forward, chin toward the chest, three times. Feel the stretch down your back, from your upper neck all the way to your tailbone. Don't strain but do stretch. Now, as you lift your head up so as not to come down onto your neck bones, tilt the head backward, chin toward the ceiling, three times. Feel the stretch down the front of your body and spine. Next, tilt the head to the right shoulder, ear toward the right shoulder, three times. Feel the stretch down the left side of your body and spine. Now tilt the head to the left shoulder, ear toward the left shoulder, three times. Feel the stretch down the right side of your body and spine. Next, circle the head in a clockwise motion, feeling this rotation all the way down your spine; do three rotations. Finally, reverse the rotation, counterclockwise, for three times. Now relax and feel the whole of your spine as one vibrant system, stretched and freely flowing with healthful spinal fluid and electrochemical energy.

Prayer of Protection

Surrounding oneself with a protective prayer is fundamental to Cayce's approach to a good meditation. He instructs us to surround ourselves with the meaning and power of the words in the prayer. Let us call on the higher forces to protect us from all negative influences, both internal and external (negative thoughts, emotions, etc.). Let the prayer words become as shields for all negative vibrations and influences. Here's a modified version of one of Cayce's protection prayers: *Now, as I approach the throne of power, might, grace, and mercy, I wrap about myself the protection found in the love for God-consciousness, in the thought of Christ Consciousness.*

Feel the meaning and power of each word and the entire statement.

Feel it surrounding you. *Imagine* it surrounding you. If you were completely conscious of God, nothing could move you, harm you, or distract you. Feel this. Imagine it. You may not have achieved it yet, but you can imagine what it will be like and its power to protect you. Wrap yourself up in this all–encompassing shield.

Prayer Words and the Spiritual Centers

Now let's look at the mechanics of this method. Assuming that we have crucified our selfish desires, conceived of our ideal, and drawn on the power and protection of the Christ, "love of God–consciousness," let's begin with prayer words for the seven chakras. These words vary with different practices, but the Cayce readings (281-29) teach that one reason the Master created the Lord's Prayer was for this purpose. As you say the prayer, feel the meaning of the italicized words as your consciousness is directed to the location of the chakra:

Our Father which art in *heaven* (the third eye center on our foreheads, and the pituitary gland), hallowed be Thy *name* (the crown chakra on the tops of our heads, and the pineal gland); Thy kingdom come, Thy *will* be done (the throat chakra, and the thyroid gland); give us this day our daily *bread* (the root chakra, which is the gonads: ovaries and testes, located at the base of our torso) and *forgive* us our debts (the solar plexus center, the adrenal glands) as we forgive our debtors; and lead us not into *temptation* (the navel chakra, the cells of Leydig), but deliver us from *evil* (the heart chakra, the thymus gland); for Thine is the *kingdom* (the throat), and the *power* (the crown of the head), and the *glory* (the forehead, third eye) forever and ever. Amen.

In reading 281-29 Cayce explains how to use this prayer:

(Q) How should the Lord's Prayer be used in this connection?
(A) As in feeling, as it were, the flow of the meanings of each portion of same throughout the body-physical. For as there is the response to the mental representations of all of these in the *mental* body, it may build into the physical body in the manner as He, thy Lord, thy Brother, so well expressed in, "I have bread ye know not of."

In one reading, Cayce gave a slightly different but interesting version of the Lord's Prayer. I found the two phrases associated with the second and fourth chakras to be more meaningful for me during the meditation.

> Our Father who art in *heaven* [forehead], hallowed be Thy *name* [crown]. Thy kingdom come. Thy *will* [throat] be done; as in heaven [head], so in earth [torso]. Give us for tomorrow the *needs* of the body [root]. Forget those trespasses as we *forgive* [solar plexus] those that have trespassed and do trespass against us. Be Thou the *guide* [navel] in the time of trouble, turmoil, and temptation. Lead us in paths of *righteousness* [heart] for thy *name's* [crown] sake. Amen.   378-44

To fully realize the power of this prayer, one must understand that it is intended to call forth the highest in each chakra. Just as we felt the words "stillness" and "God" in the earlier affirmation/mantra, so now we must feel or imagine the change brought on by these words and their meanings. Take your time. Consider this as part of the meditation period.

The order of the chakra prayer is significant in that it attempts to awaken the higher chakras before awakening the lower ones. This is the best approach. Awakening the first chakra before the seventh and sixth is like opening the serpent basket without the charm of the flute. The serpent is loose to its own interests, rather than under the charm of the higher music. Keep a higher ideal, a higher purpose, a right heart, and the consciousness focused predominantly on the higher centers. Draw the kundalini upward.

Breath Power

Now once again we take hold of the breath. This time we take a stronger hold and use it in ways that arouse the life force and draw it up through the chakras of this wonderful biospiritual instrument in which we abide. Why the breath? "*Breath* is the basis of the living organism's activity . . . This opening of the centers or the raising of the life force may be brought about by certain characters of breathing—for, as indicated, the breath is power in itself; and this power may be directed . . . " (2475-1)

Strengthening and Opening Breath

There are several breathing patterns we may use. The first is described often in the readings. It begins with a deep inhalation through the right nostril, filling the lungs and feeling strength! Then exhalation through the mouth. This should be felt throughout the torso of the body; *strength*! After three of these, shift to inhaling through the left nostril and exhaling through the right (not through the mouth). This time, feel the opening of your centers. As you do this left-right nostril breathing, keep your focus on the third eye and crown chakra, letting the other centers open toward these two. This will not be difficult, because the sixth and seventh centers have a natural magnetism, just as the snake charmer's music.

When you have finished this breathing pattern, go through the prayer again slowly, directing your attention to each chakra as you recite the phrase and key word.

Rising and Bathing Breath

Then, begin the second breathing pattern. It goes like this. Breathe through your nostrils in a normal manner; however, with each inhalation, feel or imagine the life force being drawn up from the lower parts of the torso to the crown of the head and over into the third-eye center. Hold the breath slightly, and then, as you exhale, feel or imagine the life force bathing the chakras as it descends through them to the lowest center. Pause, then inhale while again feeling or imagining the drawing upward. Repeat this cycle at a comfortable pace, using your consciousness and breath to direct the movement in synchronization with the inhalations and exhalations. As the breath and life force rise, feel or imagine how they are cleansed and purified in the higher chakras. As they descend, feel how they bathe the chakras with this purified energy. Take your time; again, consider this as part of the meditation. Do about seven cycles of inhalations and exhalations.

> These exercises [yoga breathing] are excellent . . . Thus an entity
> puts itself, through such an activity [yoga breathing], into associa-
> tion or in conjunction with all it has *ever* been or may be. For, it
> loosens the physical consciousness to the universal consciousness
> . . . Thus ye may constructively use that ability of spiritual
> attunement, which is the birthright of each soul; ye may use it as a
> helpful influence in thy experiences in the earth.   2475-1

The Rising Incantation

After this breathing pattern is a good time to use a rising incantation.
Here's one from an ancient Egyptian mystical practice described in the
readings. Breathe in deeply, then, as you very slowly exhale, direct your
consciousness to the lowest chakra and begin moving the life force upward as you chant in a drone *ah ah ah ah ah, a a a a a, e e e e e, i i i i i, o o o
o, u u u u u, m m m m m*. Each sound is associated with a chakra. "Ah" with
the root chakra (in Edgar Cayce reading 2072-10, "this is not R, but Ah,"
as the *a* in *spa*). "Ay" with the lyden center (sounds like long *a* in *able*).
"Ee" with the solar plexus (sounds like long *e* in *eve*). "I" with the heart (a
long *i*, as in *high*). "Oh" with the throat (long *o* as in *open*). "U" with the
pineal (sounds like the *u* in *true*). And "M" with the third eye (like humming the *m* in *room*).

Remember that true incanting is an inner sounding that vibrates,
stimulates, and lifts the life force. It is done in a droning manner, with a
monotonous, humming tone, vibrating the vocal cords and then directing this vibration to the chakras, thus vibrating them. Feel the chakras
being tuned to the specific sound/vibration, and then carry your consciousness upward as the sound changes. Do this chanting three or more
times or until you feel its effect. You may also want to finish this chanting portion of the practice with a few soundings of the great Om chant
(as in *home*).

Often at this point in the meditation, the head will be drawn back,
the forehead and crown may have pronounced sensations or vibrations, and the upper body and head may be moving back and forth, or

side to side, or in a circular motion. These are all natural results of the practice and are identified as such in the readings. In the Revelation, St. John associates body–shaking ("earthquakes") with the opening of the sixth chakra, followed by "silence in heaven" as the seventh chakra opens.

Into the Mind

Now we want to move in consciousness, so let the breathing and body go on autopilot (the Autonomic Nervous System will watch over them).

At this point in the practice, the whole of the body, mind, and soul is aroused and alert. Now, the ideal held is the formative influence, and development proceeds according to the ideal held.

The mind has a somewhat different experience in this type of meditation than it does in the Magic Silence method. All self–initiated activity is suspended. The mind has been changing as we have raised the energies of the body. By now it is very still yet quite alert. Stay here. Do not draw away or attempt to affect anything. Heightened expectancy and alertness is an excellent state of mind at this point. Here's where we have the greatest opportunity to receive God. Completely open your consciousness to God's. St. John says that he was "in the spirit" (the readings says this was John's way of saying that he was in meditation), and he "turned" (in consciousness) and his revelation began. St. John's word *turned* so precisely describes the cessation of all self–initiated activity. We, too, must reach a point in the meditation where we turn around from our constant outer–directed thought stream to become transfixed on God's consciousness, and purely receptive.

Expansion and the Imaginative Forces

The readings say we should have a strong sense of expansion and universality while in this state. They also recommend that we imagine expansion as we progress toward this place in the meditation. The imaginative forces should be used to help us reach higher consciousness. So, imagine expansion as you raise the life force in the early stages of the practice. According to the readings, the pineal's primary functioning is "the impulse or imaginative" force. It is the pineal chakra that aids in the transition from heightened material consciousness to real spiritual consciousness. Use your imaginative forces to aid in this transition. Also, reading 294-141 adds, "Keep the pineal gland operating and you won't grow old; you will always be young!" Again we see the rejuvenative powers of stimulating the imagination.

The Lower and Upper Gates

Edgar Cayce's reading 281-13 describes more of what occurs. "The spirit and the soul is within its encasement, or its temple within the body of the individual—see? With the arousing . . . it rises along that which is known as the Appian Way, or the pineal center, to the base of the *brain*, that it may be disseminated to those centers that give activity to the whole of the mental and physical being. It rises then to the hidden eye in the center of the brain system, or is felt in the forefront of the head, or in the place just above the real face—or bridge of nose, see?"

As we have seen, the soul is encased in the second chakra of the body, the lyden center. From this chakra it is drawn upward by the magnetism that results from stimulating the pineal center. It rises to the base of the brain and into the pineal center, the crown chakra. In ancient Egyptian mysticism, the lyden center is represented by the lower gate and the pharaoh of the lower Nile, while the pineal center is the upper gate and the pharaoh of the upper Nile. In *The Book of the Master of the Hidden Places*, there are ancient Egyptian pictures of a young man named Ani encouraging his soul to pass through the lower gate, and later Ani's soul is seen at the threshold of the upper gate, ready to make that wonderful passage into the higher consciousness. The caption under these pictures reads, "Hail ye gods who make souls to enter into their spiritual bodies. Grant ye that the soul of the reunited Ani, triumphant, may come forth before the gods, and that his soul may have peace in the Hidden Place."

A More Wonderful Life

The power gained from this type of meditation is not used to rule but to allow more of God's influence to come into our lives and into this dimension. Raising the Life Force within the body is key to higher consciousness and resurrecting mortal flesh as spiritualized flesh.

We are the channels of God in this realm, if we choose to be so. We could literally transform this realm if more of us developed ourselves to be better, clearer channels of the Life Force, the Great Spirit, God. The residual effect of this is that our individual lives become more fulfilling, abundant, rejuvenated, and eternal.

Success Is in the Doing!

From the readings' perspective, "In the doing comes the understanding," not in the talking, the reading, the believing, the knowing, or the thinking, but in the doing. So come, take up your practice. Not just to feel better, but that the infinite may manifest in the finite, lifting all to a more wonderful life!

Why Meditate?

"I just can't find time for it."
"I just don't see the value in it."
"I'm not very good at it."

Why meditate? When we feel moody, out of sorts, overworked, tired, or frustrated, why meditate? When we find ourselves whiny, or angry, or depressed, or weary, or any of the many feelings that human life brings, why meditate? When we can't quiet our minds because there are so many pressures, so many things that need attention, why meditate? When we are bored, why meditate? When we are sick or our loved one is sick, why meditate?

The answer to this question is both simple and complex, requiring some willpower and faith. The answer goes like this: As individuals, we have only a limited amount of energy, strength, wisdom, and power to effect change in our lives. As the Master asked, "Who among us, by taking thought, can change one hair on their head, or add an inch to their stature?" In the normal, human, individual condition, the answer is, "None of us." But there is another condition that we *can* get into. In the universal condition, with the spiritual influences flowing, any one of us can effect change in our lives and the lives of those around us. This is the real reason for finding time and space to meditate. As a human individual, we can do little, but as the universal forces find more presence within our minds and bodies, we become potent beings of the Life Force.

Here are a few comments about this from the Edgar Cayce readings:

> As the body-physical is purified, as the mental body is made wholly at-one with purification or purity, with the life and light within itself, healing comes, strength comes, power comes.
>
> So may an individual effect a healing, through meditation, through attuning not just a side of the mind nor a portion of the body but the *whole*, to that at-oneness with the spiritual forces within, the gift of the life force within *each* body.   281-24

"The gift of the life force [is] within each body." What a wonderful statement. Within each of us is a latent gift waiting to be claimed. It is claimed by purification of body, and the mind being wholly at-one with purity. This correlates to the passage-in-consciousness stage in which the "earthly portions" are removed from the body and suspended above it, thereby leaving the body clear, clean, pure, so the soul can rise and the spiritual influences can penetrate the whole of our being. Then comes healing, strength, and power.

> The nearer the body of an individual draws to that attunement, or consciousness . . . as is *in* the Christ Consciousness, the nearer does the body become a channel for *life—living* life—to others to whom the thought is directed. Hence at such periods, these are the manifestations of the life, or the spirit, acting *through* the body . . .
>
> Let these remain as sacred experiences, gathering more and more of same—but as such is given out, so does it come.
>
>   281-05

I particularly like the explanation that many of our deep meditation experiences are the manifestations of the life, or spirit, acting through our bodies. After all, our bodies are atomic structures:

> The body-physical is an atomic structure . . . Each atom, each cor-
> puscle, has within it the whole form of the universe—within its *own*
> structure . . . Each individual body must bring its own creative force
> in balance about each of the atomic centers in order for the resus-
> citating, revivifying to occur in the body. The law, then, is compli-
> ance with the universal spiritual influence that awakens any atomic
> center . . .   281-24

It is simply a matter of natural and divine law: If we remain in the individual, human condition, then we have limited potency in dealing with life's challenges. However, if we open ourselves regularly to the "universal spiritual influence," then human conditions are tempered by these forces—life and light—with power to make all things new.

> What moves the spirit of life's activities? *God*, but Will and Choice
> misdirect.   262-115

Meditation helps our will and choice be in accord with God's. Then life's activities move with the Divine Influence.

When is the best time to meditate? Here's a great answer from Cayce: "The best hour for meditation is 2:00 o'clock in the morning. The better [is] that set as the period in which the body and mind may be dedicated to it. Then keep thy promise to thy inner self, and to your Maker, or that to which ye dedicate thy body, mind and soul." (2982-3)

33

Cayce's Special Passage Through Dimensions of Consciousness

Of all the meditation techniques I've learned and practiced over these many years, none has been as effective as Edgar Cayce's passage–in–consciousness technique.

Here is a step–by–step guide for making passage in consciousness to God–consciousness (some of the steps have already been described in chapter 32 but are included here to retain the complete process):

1. Select a place and set aside a time for the practice. Go to that place and time daily. Allot a minimum of thirty minutes, preferably an hour.

2. Begin with stretching exercises. Stretch by reaching up high with your arms and hands while on your tiptoes. Alternate reaching to the ceiling with one hand then the other, like a cat stretching on a carpet. After a few of these stretches, bend over and touch your toes, stretching your joints, limbs, and spinal column. Continue the alternating motion with these toe–touching stretches. Now do the Cayce head–and–neck exercise: tilt your head forward, touching your chin to your chest. Feel the stretch down your back and spine as your head goes forward. Do this slowly three times. Now lift up your chin and tilt your head back three times, feeling the stretch down the front of your body and spine. Now tilt your head to the right shoulder three times, feeling the stretch

down your left side. Then tilt it to your left shoulder three times, feeling the stretch down your right side. Now rotate your head three times clockwise and then three times counterclockwise. The key is to feel the stretching all the way down your spine.

3. Now do Cayce's breathing exercise: deeply inhale through your right nostril by pressing your left nostril closed with your finger, filling your lungs and feeling strength throughout your body as you inhale. Hold the breath for a moment. Then exhale slowly and completely through your mouth. Pause with empty lungs for a moment. Then repeat the inhalation through the right nostril, filling the lungs and feeling strength. Do a total of three of these breaths. Next, inhale through the left nostril while feeling yourself opening to the Source of Life (press your right nostril closed with your finger). Hold the breath for a moment. Exhale slowly through the right nostril, not the mouth, by pressing your left nostril closed with your finger. Pause with empty lungs for a moment. Do this breath three times. During the first part of this breathing exercise (inhaling through the right nostril and exhaling through the mouth) you should feel strength. During the second part (inhaling through the left nostril and exhaling through the right nostril) you should feel an opening of the spiritual forces of the body. It's good to have fresh air in the room while doing this breathing exercise to bring more oxygen into the circulatory system and brain.

4. Now get in a relaxed position you can maintain for the whole session. If you decide to lie down, then you must cover your solar plexus with your hands (this is Cayce's instruction in 440-8). If you decide to sit up, then you do not have to be concerned with this. Place your hands wherever they are most comfortable—in your lap or on your legs, palms up or down or cupped together. It's up to you. But when lying down, you must cover your solar plexus.

5. From here on you will need your imaginative forces. Imagine the following:

Remove your *earthly portions* (Cayce's term) and personality from your body. With your mind's eye, see your mental hands moving the earthly aspects of yourself and your personality out of your body to a place in front of your body. Hold them there. You can let them back in later. For now, you are clear of them. Your body feels lighter and open, ready for your soul to come forth.

6. Now subjugate control to your soul and subconscious mind. They are perfectly capable of handling this assignment. See, feel, know your soul and subconscious mind are taking control of the system. An indication that this is occurring is a shift in your breathing, usually to deeper, steadier, slower breathing. Feel yourself turning over control to your subconscious and soul.

7. Once you feel the subjugation and deeper breathing, inspire your soul and subconscious to ascend and expand into the mind and spirit of God, the Universal Consciousness and Infinite Spirit. Use a directive suggestion such as this: Arise my soul and enter into the Presence of God, the Mind and Spirit of God, the infinite, universal consciousness of God. Feel yourself rising up; feel the expansiveness and the buoyancy of the spirit of the Source of all life. Direct yourself to become universal and infinite. Imagine it. See it. Feel it. Know it is happening.

8. Draw your head back slightly and allow your soul and subconscious mind to expand through dimensions of consciousness—upward and outwardly expanding into God's infinite presence. Keep the "movement" upward and outwardly expanding until you feel yourself becoming a part of the whole of the universal consciousness, like a drop of water becoming aware of the ocean of water within which it exists.

When you sense the infinite presence of God, connect with It. Plug into It. Hold on and maintain a connection with It. Attune yourself to the Infinite Oneness, or God. Then shift from seeking hard and guide yourself to becoming receptive to God's will. Use an affirmation such as this: "Not my will but Thy will be done in and through me." Feel God's will, God's Spirit, flowing into you. Allow it to permeate every cell of your body, every portion of your mind, every aspect of your soul. (Despite the thrill of it, you must try to subdue emotion and personalness. Stillness and universalness are necessary for ideal attunement.)

9. Once your body, mind, and soul are fully imbued with this Life Force, abide silently there. Attempt to stay conscious, or at least semiconscious. If sleep overtakes you, awaken slowly, sensing your deeper mind's perceptions rather than those of your outer mind. At first, this may be difficult. Losing consciousness, like falling asleep, is a natural tendency at this stage. But eventually, you'll be able to maintain con-

sciousness. Your breathing may be very shallow, almost not moving. Abide here. Cayce says that there is a magic in this silence. Allow that magic time to do its work.

When you sense that the session is concluding, then gradually begin to make your way back into physical life, bringing with you the spirit, energy, and essence of this attunement, this oneness with the Infinite. Feel yourself moving back into the body. Take a deep breath to aid you in drawing yourself back. Take another breath and draw the higher self back into the body and this dimension of life.

10. Now begin to balance the energies for proper functioning in physical life by equally distributing the energy throughout your body, not leaving supercharged energy in the upper portions (the head, neck, and shoulders). Imagine moving the energy to every portion of your body and mind—balanced, equally distributed. Cayce said that the internal organs of the body play a role in this balancing. Feel the energy in your lungs, liver, kidneys, intestines, glands, and skin. The brain is already full of energy. Let the energy now move from the brain to the other organs in order to regain equilibrium. This is an important step. Cayce suffered physically when he did not do this rebalancing. Take time to do it well.

11. Let your daily actions, thoughts, and words now reflect your attunement, not in a pious or better-than-thou manner, but in a natural, loving, cooperative manner. Simply practice the fruits of the spirit: love, kindness, gentleness, patience, understanding, etc.

12. Watch your dreams and intuitions. This practice will ignite dreaming. It will also generate intuitive glimpses from your deeper mind and the great collective mind that all souls are connected to. It's a good idea to carry a small note pad on which to record the insights and ideas that will come—because your outer, conscious mind (if it's anything like mine) will not be able to remember these. Like dreams, they are knowings of the deeper mind that creep through to consciousness but are hard to hold on to. The note pad and dream journal help keep them in this dimension, this outer life.

With a little practice, we can deeply attune ourselves to God and retain that spirit, energy, and essence in our daily lives.

As you can see by the technique, it does require some time. Cayce advised setting aside an hour for the practice. In the first year that I practiced this, it would take me about thirty minutes to see, feel, and know the first nine steps; now it takes about five minutes, leaving the rest of the time to be in the universal, infinite condition. Rebalancing also used to take much longer than it does now. Sometimes I would find myself an hour later still out of it and with energy in my head. Nowadays just the realization of this seems to distribute it, and my body seems to know how to do this quickly. Training. The more you practice, the more you develop your body, mind, and spirit to know and understand the finite condition and the infinite condition. There was a time when I thought I would be walking around with a glowing aura and radiating a higher vibration, but the overall experience is really quite natural and normal when balanced and integrated into your life and the whole of your being. One can be here, projected into individuality, or there, expanded into universality. After a while, even when in individuality, one can feel the universality. It's wonderful but much more natural and normal than I expected. However, Cayce always taught that it would be, saying that we were in the infinite, universal condition prior to incarnating into this dimension, this world. Therefore, returning to the other condition will not feel supernatural but natural.

I usually practice once or twice a day, in the morning and evening. Most often I practice in my bed as I'm preparing to sleep for the night. As the session ends, I let myself fall asleep. This works well, as long as I am not so tired that I cannot maintain consciousness long enough to reach oneness with God. The morning session has more energy and vitality to it, leaving me charged up for the day. Nowadays, I can complete the full process in about twenty to thirty minutes, sometimes faster. But every few days I stay in the deeper condition for an hour. It always allows the "magic silence" to better imbue me with the vitality, peace, and clarity of God's spirit and mind. It also brings out the better me, which Cayce identified as one of the main goals of meditation: "Let your better self come through."

Cayce's readings often instruct us to let God come through us into this dimension and into the lives of people around us.

Appendix

Over many years of teaching meditation, I have been asked many questions and given many answers. Perhaps some of these questions and answers may help you.

I've studied all your methods and attended your training classes, but I cannot seem to meditate. I feel like I'm sitting restlessly with myself. Nothing special is happening. It's become quite frustrating.—S.V., VA

You are correct; *you* cannot do this but your *inner* self can. You have to get your outer self out of the way, get it still and quiet, allowing your inner self to take a predominate role in the meditative experience. Try this. Get into your meditation position and then *pretend* that you have unexpectedly died. Everyone has said their good-byes, and your worldly affairs have been settled by those left behind. You are dead to this life. Now what do you do? There's nothing more you can do here. It's over. So begin to look around in your consciousness for the next life, the next realm of existence. Tell your surviving self to rise up into the heavens and find God because you've died and need to discover the next realm of activity for you. Lift yourself higher and higher into the presence of the eternal, omnipresent, loving Creator that made you. Feel, imagine, know that God exists and knows your needs and desires and wants you to succeed. Feel, imagine your soul-self rising up and expanding into the infinite, universal mind of God. Imagine it. As you begin to realize this in your imagination, in your deeper mind, connect with God; plug into God's presence and hold on. Abide there, allowing this Presence to fill you with its spirit, love, health, calm, contentment, and "peace that passes understanding." You can do this if you have died and have no other choice, so pretend that you have indeed died. This life is over and done. You have to reach up into the heavens and find the next state of consciousness, the next realm of existence. Obviously, it will be a non-physical one, and your earthly self will not be needed. Therefore, get into your nonphysical self and seek for the higher heavens and God's presence. If you really try this, you'll have better results with your meditations. It works well for me.

Some people have asked how they can be sure that they will not really die, since they are not happy here and may just decide to never come back! Cayce gives us this answer: If your soul (not your outer self, which is easily disappointed and frustrated with life) did not want to be here, it would not be here. But your soul has a purpose for this incarnation, a mission that is very important to it. Your inner self wants to overcome the forces of the egocentric self and worldliness, without condemning the world or the little self. Therefore, this incarnation, done well, is exactly what your soul is seeking. And not only your soul but the souls of those around you. We are all traveling in soul groups. Others in our lives are major players in our soul's mission this life. Meeting them and resolving karma with them is an important part of our mission. You won't really die as long as your soul still has unfinished business here and the will to finish it. Plus, once you get into God's presence, you'll feel rejuvenated and re-inspired to get back to the challenges of this life and succeed.—JVA

I love the deep teachings in the Cayce readings and other sources, but I also enjoy my friends and want to maintain our happy relationships; none of them are into this. They live normal lives and are interested in normal things. That's fine with me, but it does leave me alone, with no one to talk to about

deeper things. I'm afraid that if I begin going to meetings and events that I'll lose my "normal" relationships. I'm afraid that if I get too deeply into this, I'll be really alone. At a party the other night, I happened to mention altered states of consciousness, and one of my friends that I really like said that she didn't understand why I got into such things, and turned to speak to someone else. I felt anxious and wished that I had never brought it up. Socially, there's no room for these deep and pure thoughts. Yet, in my mind, I am urged, pulled, and called to new understanding and interpreting and perception. How can I live normally and still know and appreciate deeper thoughts about life?—J.J. e-mail

Oh will the day ever come when we can all live, love, laugh, and be happy with one another, no matter what our interests? We all want to be liked, especially by those we like and want to be with. But it doesn't always happen. Those who seek and enjoy the deeper teachings often have to "walk between the living and the dead"—meaning between those who feel the vast universal consciousness and the breadth of life and those who only seek and see the physical–material life. This is going to be a difficult balancing act for you. As you indicate, the more you get into this stuff, the more you're going to separate yourself from those who only live the material life. The only bridging force that I've found for such situations is love. If the ultimate goal is to love God and others, then it really doesn't matter if someone is into altered states of consciousness or not, does it? If they are loving, kind, considerate, sharing, giving, forgiving, and patient, then they are practicing the fruits of the spirit. Yet you will still have to be careful with your pearls. We cannot expect others to immediately know the value of our pearls if they have no appreciation of things beyond the physical–material. We have to be patient with them. We also have to keep our shields up in order to avoid being hurt by insensitive comments and slights. It's just the way things are.

I would suggest that you set aside time for yourself and your interests. Otherwise, you'll not be fully growing into your potential. This does mean that they may come to know what you're into and judge you harshly for it, even snubbing you. But you cannot deny your inner longings without serious consequences to your psyche. It's the price we all have to pay.

Nevertheless, try to balance these two worlds as long as you can. In my case, I have dear relationships with people who have no interest whatsoever in my stuff, but they like me and I like them. Our lives meet over other interests and activities. And it's good. But through the years some friends have chosen to drop me from their circle of connections. As much as it hurt, it was probably for the best—for each of us.

But these times are seeing the merging of many heretofore opposites: religion and science, mysticism and physics, healing and medicine, so there's hope for friendships too.—JVA

I'm having a difficult time finding something to do that makes my soul happy while paying the bills. You seem to be doing both. Can you give me any help? How does one get into this field and make enough money to survive?—R.A., NY

This is a good question and one that has been asked many times, from ancient times to today. Even Edgar Cayce was asked, "How can I put my finances in order so that I can devote my life to psychic development and spiritual growth?" Cayce's answer went something like this: *It is not by separating these two aspects of life that the greater growth occurs but by uniting them. Use your psychic and spiritual abilities to solve your material needs. In this manner does the greater growth occur.* Developing one's spiritual and psychic talents and connections is critical to success.

Now let me answer this question from my own personal perspective, as one who has spent much of his life attempting to do what you are asking. In looking back (hindsight is 20/20), I would say that one has to be really drawn to do this or have a calling to do it. Why? Because it is so painfully difficult for the normal, physically oriented person and all those who depend upon that person for material stability. I speak from experience! Also, this way is so paradoxically ethereal and material that it is a rare person who can blend both and keep sane. It depends so much upon the nonmaterial, unseen forces for sustenance and support that one has to be willing to budget the time and effort it takes to work with meditation and dreams and endure a long development stage (at least in my case), in which many misunderstandings and misinterpretations occur. Yet, at the same time, it requires a good knowledge of traditional business practices in order to correctly give what others want while receiving in turn what one needs in order to give again. It's a very hard way to go through life. In my case, I was born with Neptune in the second house! My material sustenance was destined to be through watery, ethereal means, whether I liked it or not.

If you decide that you want to go this way, keep the day job for a while. You'll need it. Occasionally you'll need it again, and maybe again. Soul work is better done as an avocation than a vocation. Begin with little opportunities in the evenings and on the weekends. Listen carefully to what others say about their needs and interests and your presentations. As you develop, know that you'll never get to a place that the work is done and you are a success. You are only as good as your last presentation; and word-of-mouth is very fast to spread your gifts or weaknesses.—JVA

Does loneliness have to be among the things we must "long-suffer" on the spiritual path? I don't see why our lives have to be so separate and lonely. It's not that I don't have friends who believe in the things we do, but I don't have any intimate companions to share life with. My brother and sister think I'm a little crazy. They live a normal material life, with all the material goals and activities that don't interest me. The men I meet are just not right for me. Does it have to be this way?—M.L., e-mail

In most cases, a little loneliness is indeed a portion of every soul's journey—"Yea though I walk through the valley of the shadow of death [alone], Thou art with me." This "valley" is not just physical death, of course, but represents the many deaths we each experience in life, from the death of childhood dreams to lifelong relationships. It also represents each night's sleep; sleep being a shadow of death too. In some cases, there is a karmic dynamic to present loneliness, and one simply has to meet this with patience and some humor. In all cases, the soul must come to know and experience that God, the Great Spirit, the Universal Consciousness, is the soul's ultimate companion. In achieving this, the soul learns that the second commandment (Love one another) is an integral part of the first commandment (Love God with all your being). Not only God is God, but all of these others and ourselves are a part of that Oneness. Cayce recommended that if we want companionship, we need to be a companion to others, and keep up our efforts to be a good friend.—JVA

I have read something you wrote in regard to meditation that a person should not leave too much energy in their head. I have been doing a kundalini type meditation similar to the Golden Flower method that you wrote about, and I do have trouble afterwards with a feeling of too much energy in my head. However, I don't know how to change it. Would you please give me some ideas for getting it distributed more evenly in my body?— E.W., e-mail

Three ways: First, as the meditation is concluding, visualize sending the energy to others on your prayer list (Cayce recommends that you "see" the other person surrounded with the Light and energy you've raised). Second, use your *imaginative forces* (Cayce's term) to move and distribute the energies throughout your body by visualization and "feeling." Third, use your breath to redistribute the energy after the meditation as you used it to gather the energy for the meditation, by taking deep breaths; and as you exhale, feel the energy going out of your head and neck to other parts of your body. If the energy is still too much in your head and neck, you can actually do this again many minutes or hours after the meditation. On the other hand, if you find yourself low on energy during the day, simply pause and begin taking deep breaths to draw your energy up from the lower chakras to the higher, unite with the Infinite energy of God, and then bathe the body in this revitalized energy as you exhale. Breath is life.—JVA

Since the 23rd Psalm is recommended by Cayce to end a meditation and close the chakras, is there a direct correlation be-

tween keywords and the chakras, as Cayce gave for the Lord's Prayer?—B.D., GA

Actually, I am not aware of any instruction in the actual Cayce readings that gives the 23rd Psalm as a closing device for meditation. As far as I know, this became a common practice throughout the A.R.E. community because Hugh Lynn Cayce loved it so much and regularly suggested it. It has now become a tradition, a good tradition, in my opinion.

Now, as to the correlating of keywords to the chakras, which Cayce's readings do give for the Lord's Prayer, there are also no readings on this for the 23rd Psalm. However, inspired by your question, I attempted to meditate deeply and see if I could find some correlation. The following is what came to me. But each of us should find the keywords for ourselves. What works for me may be different for you and others.

"The Lord is my shepherd [pituitary, third eye]; I shall not want. He maketh me to lie down in green pastures [pineal, crown]; He leadeth me beside still waters [thyroid, throat]. He restoreth my soul [inner, true self]. He leadeth me in the paths of righteousness [thymus, heart] for his name's sake [pineal, crown]. Yea, though I walk through the valley [gonads, root] of the shadow of death [adrenals, solar plexus], I will fear no evil [cells of leydig, navel]; for thou [pituitary, third eye] art with me. Thy rod [standards, ideals] and thy staff [kundalini, life force], they comfort me. Thou preparest a table [four lower chakras restored] before me in the presence of mine enemies [lower urges]. Thou hast anointed my head [pineal, crown] with oil; my cup [pituitary, third eye] runneth over. Surely goodness and mercy [four lower chakras spiritualized] shall follow me all the days of my life; And I shall dwell in the house [the head, three upper chakras] of the Lord for ever."

Let me explain some of my correlates. Rather than selecting Lord as the keyword in the psalm for the third eye, I found the word *shepherd* felt better for me. Few people know that, from the line in the Lord's Prayer, "Our Father which art in heaven," Cayce actually gave the word *heaven* as the third-eye keyword, not *Father*. But the study group working with him changed the keyword to *Father*, and it has been published that way for years. The selection of *green pastures* for the pineal was easy, but *still waters* for the throat chakra was a bit of a surprise to me. However, during my meditation, the words had a profound effect upon my throat chakra. As we all know, Cayce associates the throat chakra with the keyword *will* in the Lord's Prayer. I felt that when I seek God's will over my own, I am abiding in the still waters. It worked for me. See what works for you.

Perhaps the most surprising guidance in my meditation was the collective keywords. *Table* felt like my entire lower centers, as did *goodness and mercy*. It felt as though my lower, earthly centers had become united and spiritualized. The "house of the Lord" was an easy correlate with the head chakras because the Taoist text *Secret of the Golden Flower* has a beautiful metaphor that has stuck with me over the years: "In the square inch field inside the square foot house, life can be regulated." The "square inch field" is the pituitary, which abides within the "square foot house" of the head. As you know, Cayce's readings stated that the four lower chakras are "earth," and the three upper chakras are "heaven" in the Lord's Prayer. I felt that some of that grouping was occurring within the 23rd Psalm as well.

I enjoyed this meditation so much I'll be doing it again. I've always felt that the 23rd Psalm had profound mystical implications for the meditator, but I've never attempted to explore these. Thanks for asking such a good question.—JVA

I've come to see meditation in two different ways. I used to see it as this huge, serious mind–changing experience—it was supposed to be the ultimate experience; however, I couldn't ever achieve that. I felt like I was searching for something that I didn't know. Now I see it as getting in touch with my body, calming it down to better see things as they are supposed to be. It's more of a calming technique, and this works. Was I wrong to think of it as a mind–altering thing or is that a rare experience, such as Buddha's enlightenment under the Bodhi tree?—A.V., e–mail

As far as I'm concerned, you're right on both accounts. Meditation is a wonderful tool for calming the body and body–self to see life better and allow the better you to come through each day, in each situation. It is also a tool for having an occasional enlightenment experience. Keep on keeping on.—JVA

I have been hearing voices. They seem nice enough, but is this okay? It started about a year ago. Are these the guides that everyone talks about? Or am I possessed? Sometimes I don't feel like myself, like I may be going crazy. Can you give me some advice? If I wanted to stop hearing the voices, how would I do this? Please don't use my name.—e-mail

Just from the general tone of your words, I'd say that you need to stop the voices and seek only God's Spirit, God's Presence. All souls, all beings, all creatures exist in free-willed dimensions of life, as you do. Therefore, no being or guide is as important to you and your soul as your Maker. Seek only the direct, personal, loving guidance of your Maker, the Maker of all things, all beings. How do you do this? Well, it depends on just how overwhelming these voices are. If they are strong and you cannot easily shut them out, then you need to use the Cayce radio-active- or wet-cell appliance with gold chloride in the solution jar. Call A.R.E. for the phone numbers and addresses of those who sell these items (1-800-333-4499). You'll also need to watch your diet. Eat more healthfully and avoid alcohol or any drugs that alter your consciousness. Fast your thoughts and entertainment viewing. Do not watch any emotionally challenging shows (horror, possession, etc.). Get massages and adjustments from practitioners with the best vibes for you. Exercise your body daily. Feel yourself regaining control over your muscles, nerves, and fluids. You will also need to increase your praying, especially before sleep or meditation—actually, you should stop meditating for a little while, until you feel more in control of yourself. Use Cayce's surrounding prayer of protection all day long: "As I seek to approach the Throne of Power, Might, Grace, and Mercy, I wrap about myself the protection found in the Christ Consciousness, in the love for God-consciousness." Mean this! And then seek only God-consciousness. Keep God in your mind and heart all day. Push away any thoughts that are not about God, God's children, your communication with God's children (those around you in your life), and your Maker's love and concern for you. Let only God guide you.—JVA

In your Kundalini–Raising tape, you say the Egyptian high priest Ra–Ta used certain techniques to make himself younger over a period of seven years. What are these techniques?—R.S., e–mail

While in meditation, he had a musician play the seven notes of the scale, attuning his chakras to the notes. On some days, the musician used a wind instrument; on others, a stringed instrument. He also had a powerful purpose for which to be rejuvenated: he wanted to join with Hermes to build the Great Pyramid of Giza for humanity in accord with God's will and plan. The calling helps the music.—JVA

When I meditate, I get pressure in my head. It's uncomfortable. Sometimes it is inside my head. Other times, it's at my temples or forehead—the third eye, I guess, right? It can leave me with a headache all day. Am I doing something wrong? Is there any way to alleviate this?—K.T., MO

Well, most meditators do feel some pressure in their head, but yours sounds a bit too much. I don't believe that we should experience headaches as a result of meditation, so I would recommend that you make some changes. First, make sure you do the head–and–neck exercises before and after your meditations. Second, at some point in your meditation, take some deep breaths (about three) and imagine or feel a *rising* sensation as you inhale. As you exhale, imagine all of this raised energy moving throughout every portion of your body. This includes all your extremities, to your fingertips and toes, but also all of your *inner* organs (liver, kidneys, lungs, intestines, and so on). As you exhale, feel yourself relaxing and releasing all the tension and energy into a glowing peacefulness. As you feel this relaxation and peacefulness growing, stop the deep breaths and let your breathing go back to a gentle automatic breathing. Relax, and sit in this relaxation for a little while. Do not leave any tension in your head, neck, or shoulders. Imagine it flowing gently down into your whole body, equally distributed and balanced. I hope this helps.—JVA

**In our study group we had a lengthy discussion about a sec-
tion in your book *Jesus: His Words Decoded, His Mystery Teachings
Revealed*, which we are studying and enjoying each week. In
chapter 18, on "Spirit and Soul," you write: "Cayce says that it
(spirit–soul) is 'a thing apart from anything earthy,' and does
not descend into the realms of earth unless we lift ourselves up
to it and connect with it." I had trouble putting this statement
into my own words, and we discussed what it means at great
length. Again, on page 101: "The spirits of all that have passed
from the physical plane remain about the plane until their development carries them onward or are returned (reincarnated)
for their development here." Does the spirit return to its Source
but the soul remain in the earth plane until it is ready to go on
into another incarnation or another realm? It seems to me that
the Spirit would have to remain in the soul for it to be vital or
even a "living soul" on another level. And how would we "lift
up" to bring the Spirit down into the earth realm? Life itself in
any form must have the Spirit in it from the first, right? These
phrases are confusing. Any comments that you think might
clarify the first question, in particular, would be greatly appreciated. Blessings, M.B.—LA**

You and I are using the term *spirit* in two different ways: one to indicate the "life force," which must always be with the soul and the body-
self in order for it to live, and the other to indicate the godling portion
of our nature, which abides in higher dimensions of consciousness. The
spirit, in the sense of the godling-self made in the image of God, is the
"thing apart from anything earthly." The spirit, in the sense of the life
force, is with us always.

Let's look at your questions individually: "Does the spirit return to its
Source but the soul remain in the earth plane until it is ready to go on
into another incarnation or another realm?" No. They are not separate
but rather in different dimensions of consciousness.

"It seems to me that the Spirit would have to remain in the soul for it
to be vital or even a 'living soul' on another level." Now you're using
spirit to mean the life force. Yes, the life force must remain with every

aspect of our being in order for it to have life. But the godling portion of our being may be in a different dimension of consciousness than our soul portion—a portion that Cayce described as being similar to our personal self but much bigger—he called it our *individuality*.

"Life itself in any form must have the Spirit in it from the first, right?" Here you're using *spirit* to mean the life force rather than the godling-self made in the image of God. Yes, life in any form must have the Spirit in it from the first. But the spirit-self, the godling portion, may be in dimensions of consciousness far beyond the soul-self and even farther beyond the material, earthly self. If we lift our consciousness up, then we may unite with our spirit-self, our godling nature.—JVA

Please give me your insight on why I feel a coldness or like a slight cool whiff on my right side when I meditate. I feel it on my face and sometimes farther down on my right hand. Any thoughts you have on this would be appreciated.—S.T., e-mail

Edgar Cayce was asked a similar question by one of the members (number 993, Florence Edmonds, a good healer) of the prayer and healing group, the Glad Helpers. He told her that this was "the breath of an angel, or the breath of a master"! Wow! But don't get distracted by this phenomenon. Even the angel or master would want you to focus on the Source of all life, not on the angel/master's presence. But it is a wonderful side effect of good meditation. Enjoy. Here's that reading I referred to:

> (Q) [993]: On several occasions while meditating with the group there was a cool feeling as if mentholatum had been placed upon my head and forehead, extending down upon the nose.
> (A) As would be termed—literal—as the breath of an angel, or the breath of a master. As the body attunes self, as has been given, it may be a channel where there may be even *instant* healing with the laying on of hands. The more often this occurs the more *power* is there felt in the body, the forcefulness in the act or word.
>
> 281-5

I read your article on the A.R.E. web site that you wrote on the kundalini. How can I get more on meditation and the kundalini?—G., e-mail

That's a good question. I suppose Edgar Cayce would have answered, "From within yourself," and he would have been right on. I occasionally write more on meditation and the kundalini in my newsletters. I have received several e-mails lately that have asked where to get my schedule of speaking and touring. You can get these in the A.R.E. membership magazine, *Venture Inward*, the A.R.E. web site *edgarcayce.org*, and my web site *johnvanauken.com*.—JVA

It seems to me that souls would still have areas of growth and progression even after the enlightenment experience (that so many experience at death). Can you recommend any Cayce readings on what happens to the enlightened souls after death? For example, is the "Communion of Saints" made up of enlightened souls?—Thanks, Don C., Fountain Valley, CA

Good Question. Here's Cayce's comment:

> There is only *one* Spirit—of Truth. There may be divisions, as there may be many drops of water in the ocean, yet they are all of the ocean. Separated, they are named for those activities in various spheres of experiences. The communion of the spirit of the divine within self may be with the source of divinity. This is what is meant by the communion of saints, of those that are of one thought; for all thought for activity emanates from the same source, and there is the natural communion of those who are in that thought.   262-87

There are many realms of activity—in the earth and beyond it in heavenly realms. Throughout them all is one, inseparable essence. That essence is the Life Force, God. Wherever we are, we can unite with that Oneness. There is no real death, only beyond-the-body activity. It is difficult for the 3-D portion of our being to describe these other realms in terms that can be understood three-dimensionally. Hence we do not have a clear 3-D idea of how life is like beyond matter. However, we know this intuitively because we have all experienced it.—JVA

I'm having some trouble with the final stages of your Passage In Consciousness technique. When I get to the part where you're supposed to say "Not my will, but Thy will be done," the meditation seems to slow down and drift. What am I doing wrong?—e-mail

From your further comments, which I do not have room to publish, I know that you are doing well with the rest of the practice, so let's assume that your difficulty is with the words "Not my will, but Thy will be done" and the meaning behind them. There are two reactions to these words; you'll have to determine which is yours:

1. When some people say these words, they become uncomfortable because they fear losing control and worry that they cannot handle the outcome of such an open receptivity to God's will. In this case, we need to develop faith and trust in God and God's love for us, wanting only the best for us. Of course, God's perspective on what is good for us may be a bit different than ours, and we must be prepared to make some adjustments, knowing that, in the end, we will be better off for it.

2. When others say these words, they become so passive that they do nothing, leaving the whole experience up to the Lord; the Lord has to come and take over, leading them into the light. But Cayce's readings have taught us that we are cocreators with God, not servants or automatons. God seeks to work *with* us, not *for* us. Passivity is not what we need at this moment in the meditation. We need "active patience," as Cayce called it. We need to be *expectant*. We also need to use our imaginative forces to help us perceive God's presence and feel God's energies uniting with ours. At the moment that we sense this union, then we want God's will to guide us, show us the better way, and make us the best person we *can* be.

Try this and see if it helps.—JVA

I have just recently located all this wonderful information online [http://www.edgarcayce.org/ps2/]. My comment or

question is: As I stated, I have been using TM for over 30 years now. I love it. At a certain time of the day, I get a calling. I can't explain it but I feel it. I know it. Wherever I am, whatever I'm doing, I have to stop as soon as I can and go to my quiet place. I sit in peace and repeat my mantra, and soon I will drift off to a time and place or something else. When I arise, sometimes I wonder where I think I just was or what I may have seen or heard.

I feel close and refreshed and ready to take on the world as soon as my blood starts moving again.

I have never had any advance training in my TM program, but I have continued to use it now since 1974, when I was compelled to step inside a small townhouse meeting where two brothers were giving a seminar on the program. I never heard of it prior to the evening.—J.F. e-mail

Thank you for sharing this. Yes, meditation—and almost any method of it—makes a big difference in our lives and in our physical, emotional health and well-being. As I read your comments, I had a strong feeling that your soul has meditated in past lives, because it comes so naturally to you and the "calling" is an inner message from your soul. I, too, have been meditating for a long time, nearly 40 years! Honestly, I wouldn't be half the person I am today if I had not learned and practiced meditation throughout the many stages of my life and life's many challenges. Thanks again for sharing your experiences.—JVA

A.R.E. PRESS

The A.R.E. Press publishes books, videos, and audiotapes meant to improve the quality of our readers' lives—personally, professionally, and spiritually. We hope our products support your endeavors to realize your career potential, to enhance your relationships, to improve your health, and to encourage you to make the changes necessary to live a loving, joyful, and fulfilling life.

For more information or to receive a free catalog, call:

800–333–4499

Or write:

A.R.E. Press
215 67th Street
Virginia Beach, VA 23451–2061

EDGAR CAYCE'S A.R.E.

What Is A.R.E.?

The Association for Research and Enlightenment, Inc., (A.R.E.©) was founded in 1931 to research and make available information on psychic development, dreams, holistic health, meditation, and life after death. As an open-membership research organization, the A.R.E. continues to study and publish such information, to initiate research, and to promote conferences, distance learning, and regional events. Edgar Cayce, the most documented psychic of our time, was the moving force in the establishment of A.R.E.

Who Was Edgar Cayce?

Edgar Cayce (1877–1945) was born on a farm near Hopkinsville, Ky. He was an average individual in most respects. Yet, throughout his life, he manifested one of the most remarkable psychic talents of all time. As a young man, he found that he was able to enter into a self–induced trance state, which enabled him to place his mind in contact with an unlimited source of information. While asleep, he could answer questions or give accurate discourses on any topic. These discourses, more than 14,000 in number, were transcribed as he spoke and are called "readings."

Given the name and location of an individual anywhere in the world, he could correctly describe a person's condition and outline a regiment of treatment. The consistent accuracy of his diagnoses and the effectiveness of the treatments he prescribed made him a medical phenomenon, and he came to be called the "father of holistic medicine."

Eventually, the scope of Cayce's readings expanded to include such subjects as world religions, philosophy, psychology, parapsychology, dreams, history, the missing years of Jesus, ancient civilizations, soul growth, psychic development, prophecy, and reincarnation.

A.R.E. Membership

People from all walks of life have discovered meaningful and life–transforming insights through membership in A.R.E. To learn more about Edgar Cayce's A.R.E. and how membership in the A.R.E. can enhance your life, visit our web site at EdgarCayce.org, or call us toll-free at 800–333–4499.

Edgar Cayce's A.R.E.
215 67th Street
Virginia Beach, VA 23451–2061

EDGARCAYCE.ORG